TERRY FOX
Fashion
COLLECTION

TERRY FOX
Fashion
COLLECTION

10 COUTURE GARMENTS TO MAKE
FROM START TO FINISH

Trafalgar Square Publishing

NORTH POMFRET, VERMONT

I would like to dedicate this book to my fiancé, Rob, and
thank him for his continuing loyal support during the
construction of the *Terry Fox Fashion Collection*.

First published in the United States of America in 1995 by
Trafalgar Square Publishing, North Pomfret, Vermont 05053

First published in Great Britain in 1994 by
Anaya Publishers Ltd, London

Text copyright © Terry Fox 1994
Photography and illustrations
copyright © Anaya Publishers 1994

Editors: Julie Watkins and Rosemary Wilkinson
Designer: Nigel Partridge
Photographer: Huggy of Premier Photographic
Stylist: David Evans
Hair Stylist: Michel Eddery
Make-up: Emma Kotch
Pattern artwork: Rick Sullivan
Pattern cutter: Jan Tordoff
Technique illustrations: Terry Evans
Template artwork: Anthony Duke

The Publishers would like to thank Premier Photographic,
London and Los Angeles, Elite Premier models, Storm models
and L.A. models for their help with the photography. Also
special thanks to Johnny Gold, the proprietor of Tramp night
club and the Belvedere, Holland Park, for his invaluable help
with the locations.

ISBN 1-57076-016-0
Library of Congress Catalog Card Number: 94-60998

Typeset in Great Britain by Servis Filmsetting Ltd, Manchester
Colour reproduction by HBM Print Pte Ltd, Singapore
Printed and bound in Singapore by CS Graphics Pte Ltd

KEY TO PATTERN PIECES

☐	Each square represents 2.5cm (1in), with thicker lines every 5cm (2in)
•	Denotes start or finish of stitching line or matching point with another pattern piece
▲	Notch
■	Position of snap fastener
⊢●⊣	Button/buttonhole position
↕	Straight grain
..........10	Size 10 pattern line
———12	Size 12 pattern line
- - - - - 14	Size 14 pattern line
_ . _ . _	Cutting line for lining
---gather---	Gathering line

All pattern pieces include a 15mm (⅝in) seam allowance
unless otherwise stated.

All pattern pieces are reduced to one sixth of the
original size.

Note: When laying out pattern pieces on fabric before
cutting out, make sure that the pieces are on the straight
of the grain as indicated by the arrows or on the fold of
the fabric. Do not follow the layout of the pieces on the
page grid.

CONTENTS

INTRODUCTION

*M*y entire working life has revolved around sewing in one form or another; from fashion college, through the workrooms of Zandra Rhodes and the Emmanuels, to my own label collection retailing in such prestigious outlets as the London department store, Harrods.

Despite this success, I have found greater satisfaction over the last four years in sharing my knowledge and passion for sewing with others of a similar mind: in the classroom, seminar or even among customers at a favourite fabric stall in my home town. This book has been written with the aim of spreading that knowledge even further.

Don't be put off by my designer background, or intimidated by the word *couture*. I've come to realize that the most important element of successful dressmaking is confidence. Yes, you can achieve a couture look, time and time again, using the simple and straightforward techniques described in the following pages. Apply them to the *Terry Fox Fashion Collection* or any other pattern you care to use.

Follow the techniques with confidence. Sewing is a wonderful pastime and I hope you'll find more than a little inspiration to give you the couture finish you've always longed for.

Happy sewing!

Terry Fox

BEFORE YOU BEGIN . . .

*W*elcome to couture dressmaking! Before you begin making any of the garments, please take the time to absorb the following tips and information to enable you to get the very best from this book and your couture dressmaking.

This book has been written with the intention of providing you with inside knowledge, knowledge that will ensure couture results every time you sew. It is not just a step-by-step guide to ten different garments; the designs are there to illustrate techniques which can and should be applied to any dressmaking pattern. Some techniques you may only use once in a lifetime for that extra special occasion; others you will use time and time again on outfits for every day wear.

The designs are also quite flexible. In some cases you can economize on fabrics and time by using fewer layers and omitting the embellishments. Adapt the finished look of each garment for your own personal needs, if you wish. For example, the two ballgowns featured could easily be made in white or ivory for a unique bridal gown.

THE PATTERNS

All patterns have been graded to size 10, 12 and 14. Please use care when transferring and cutting out the pattern, ensuring that you follow the correct size lines at all times. Measurements are given below for each size.

Note: American pattern sizes will differ from ready-to-wear garments. Select your dress size according to the measurements given below.

METRIC (centimetres)			
American/UK	10	12	14
European	36	38	40
Bust	83	87	92
Waist	64	67	71
Hips	88	92	97
Nape to waist	40.5	41.5	42

IMPERIAL (inches)			
American/UK	10	12	14
European	36	38	40
Bust	32½	34	36
Waist	25	26½	28
Hips	34½	36	38
Nape to waist	16	16¼	16½

If your measurements do not correspond, select the bust size closest to your own. It is easier to adjust the waist and hips than the upper body area (see Fitting below). Beginners in dressmaking should seek experienced help in enlarging the patterns to different body measurements. Remember, you don't have to make exactly the same garment to get the most from this book. You can be equally successful using a commercial pattern of similar style and adding the techniques and embellishment ideas that you will find in the following pages.

All the patterns have been reduced to a sixth of the original size. They can be enlarged back to full size by using either a photocopier with an enlarging facility (many commercial outlets now offer an enlarging service) or by transferring to dressmakers' graph paper, which can be found in any good haberdashery department.

Each square on the pattern grid represents 2.5cm (1in) with thicker lines every 5cm (2 in). To enlarge a pattern piece first mark out the total number of squares required in pencil on your graph paper (*fig.1*).

FIG 1

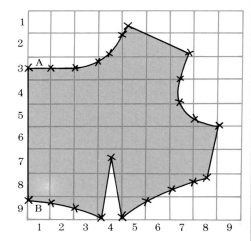

If the pattern piece has a straight line or edge it is advisable to mark this first, for example, the centre front in fig.1 (line AB). From this line you can then carefully count the squares, up, down and across to mark the next points. Mark out all the prominent points first, such as waistline, centre front, shoulder etc. Pay particular attention to grainlines and the multi-sizing; you must be accurate in following the correct size line. Using a ruler you can now join up the straight lines between two points. For curved areas you will need to plot or mark on each square the precise point at which the pattern line crosses it. For sleeves you may find it easier to divide the pattern up into sections.

Once all the outline is complete, ensure that you transfer all the symbols, buttonholes and straight grainlines. When you are happy with the pattern outline, you can ink in the lines, using a colourfast pen to avoid staining.

The seam allowance for all garments will be 15mm (⅝in) unless otherwise stated. The hem allowance is marked on each individual pattern. Be sure to read the entire construction notes for any garment before starting work to ensure you have all requirements to hand. Most, if not all, of the general sewing notions required are detailed below.

COUTURE TECHNIQUES

At the beginning of each project there is a list of the methods and techniques used in the making up of that particular garment. These techniques will always be found in the Couture Techniques section, starting on page 108. These fully illustrated techniques cover everything from bound buttonholes to zigzag seams.

All the stitches which have been used in the book, from backstitch to zigzag stitch, are detailed and illustrated on pages 122 and 123.

FABRIC DEFINITIONS

These are given on page 124 since it is appreciated that some fabric names may vary from country to country. The guide will assist readers in obtaining the same types or similar fabrics as those used in the book.

One other little tip; I usually use tacking or basting solely to secure interlining layers together. I will nearly always use pins to transfer pattern markings such as darts to the fabric and to temporarily hold sections together before stitching.

INTERLINING/UNDERLINING

This, to me, is the inside secret to making the outside of any garment work!

For that couture finish, you need to look behind the scenes at the couture workshop and the secret techniques used there. There could be as many as fifteen different layers in one gown, if that design requires a certain effect. Don't let that frighten you. Once you understand the theory behind interlinings and you know what's available, anything goes! I use approximately forty different interlinings, combining several in any one garment.

Obviously there are a few ground rules to follow, such as matching laundering and fibre content. But there is no definite right or wrong. You can do whatever you wish to achieve the desired effect, and only you, the wearer, designer or dressmaker, can really know what that is.

WHAT IS THE DIFFERENCE BETWEEN INTERLINING AND INTERFACING?

Interfacings are necessary to the construction of a garment to support the shape in specific areas. Commercial patterns usually recommend interfacings on collars, cuffs, facings etc. Recommendations for interlinings are not common, but couture houses will use them in every conceivable part of a garment to form a solid foundation. Interlinings form a second skin or skeleton and are always worked as one

layer with the main fabric. If it works for them, it can work for you too! It only requires a little thought, a needle, thread and pair of hands.

WHY SHOULD I INTERLINE?

1. *Body*. This is perhaps the most common reason. Interlining will give structure and maintain a shape, such as sleeves, drapes, bows and over-skirts.

2. *Density*. You can add density to certain fabrics to eliminate shadowing caused by the seams, darts and facings. The white bridal gown is relentless in allowing the insides to show through. Gone is that professional finish when hemlines, seams and pockets show through. A closely woven interlining will block these and add depth of colour.

3. *Finish*. The interlining not only eliminates shadowing, but also the ridges caused by seams and facing edges resting against the main fabric. Once the raw edge is behind two, three or even four layers, we have a much smoother, even finish.

4. *Creasing*. Some of the most beautiful fabrics are natural fibres; silk, wool, cotton and linen, but they all crease, making them a no-go area for many of us. A carefully chosen interlining can help to control creasing by adding a spring or softness.

5. *Seating*. Open-weave fabrics, such as the super Chanel tweeds or Lagerfeld wool and silk mixes, are now more readily available to the home dressmaker. However, they can seat terribly once worn. A light but tightly woven interlining, such as pure silk organza, can prevent this.

6. *Fraying*. Loosely-woven fabrics have a tendency to fray, but anchored to an interlining loose ends are secure and less likely to be a problem.

7. *Foundation*. By virtue of the way it supports the main fabric, the interlining can be used to secure hems and facings without any stitching showing through to the outside. No more facings rolling to the right side of the garment; gently push them to the wrong side and prickstitch in place without any stitches showing in the main fabric. For

anything you feel that needs a secure stitch or two, simply use the interlining.

8. *Changing characteristics of the main fabric*. Have you ever bought the most wonderful piece of fabric only to find it won't work with the pattern or design you have chosen? Don't despair. You can control and change the characteristics of the fabric by totally interlining with a different fabric, or combining a selection of layers.

Unfortunately there are no hard and fast combination rules for main fabric and interlining fabric. It very much depends on the individual design and the type of garment you are making. Every garment has to be considered individually. It's really a process of elimination until you find the finish you want. For all the garments in the book I have included reasons for the use of the different interlining layers. This will give you an idea of the different combinations available and can be used as a starting point for your own experiments. Whatever interlinings you use, I can promise that you will be amazed at the instant results!

APPLYING INTERLININGS

Cut out all main fabric pieces. Choose the interlining fabric and then cut out these pieces. Take each corresponding pattern piece and mount the two together (usually wrong sides together). Tack the two fabrics together using a long, fine needle to enable you to push more fabric onto the needle and thus do the job more quickly.

Tack with an even 13mm (½in) running stitch, 13mm (½in) from the raw edge. This stitching line will not then interfere with the machined seam line, or allow movement between the layers. Treat the two layers as one for all construction methods, including darts and seams.

Don't be tempted to cheat and machine the layers together. You will probably be working with different fibres which may cause slippage under the machine. Tack and smooth as you go to ensure that the layers lie flat to each other.

FITTING

This is an essential area to spend time on. There is so much work involved in making these garments that it would be a shame to spoil them with a less than perfect fit. I would like to make it easier for you and simply say add 5cm (2in) to your bust and hip measurements for a perfect fit. Unfortunately, that is not the case. Only you know the degree of ease which you need and prefer in your garments, whether it be tight or loose fitting. Commercial patterns have ease or tolerance built in, but until you have the finished garment to wear, it is difficult to know how much ease you personally prefer or need. That is why I strongly recommend the use of a toile!

A toile is a mock-up of the finished garment, traditionally made from calico. As this fabric is available in various weights you need to choose something close to your chosen fabric, so that you can see the real finished effect.

I am the worst person for testing and trying; I always want to get started on the idea and that beautiful fabric straight away. But I strongly urge you to take the time, which may ultimately save you more time and money, to see if the garment will fit and suit you.

From a toile you may decide to move seams to flatter your shape, lift a waistline to give height, take fullness from a skirt and so on. It's so easy to just add more to the seam allowance to make up for the few pounds which may have crept on, but what if you are round-shouldered or hollow-backed? We are round people, with curves, lumps and bumps. The only way to get a flat piece of fabric around the body is to mould it in a 3-dimensional way. Nobody has the same figure shape as a commercial dressmaking pattern and once the fabric is cut, it is usually too late to rectify a poor fit. So many times I have seen dressmakers trying to pull up shoulders or pull down hems to release wrinkling, but it just doesn't work. Your body shape tells you where it needs the fit and any problem areas will easily show up at the toile stage.

Write detailed notes all over the toile with a bold fibre pen. The toile will eventually become your new pattern. Start the process like this.

1. Before cutting out the toile take some of your basic measurements and make any obvious changes to the paper pattern. Guidelines for measuring are given below.

2. Transfer the amended pattern to the calico with all necessary markings. You will not need facings. Pin and cut out.

Try not to cheat by only making up part or half of the garment. It is rare to find a figure shape with identical halves! You need to have a full, clear picture of balance and how the entire garment will sit. You cannot do this if there is no ballgown skirt attached to the bodice!

3. Machine stitch all the seams together. Set in the sleeves and skirt. Use a large coloured stitch on your machine to make it easier when dismantling the toile.

4. Now you can fit the toile to your personal shape. Put in, or take out, extra fabric. Pinch together any excess fabric and pin; cut through the toile in tight areas to see how much extra ease is required. Adjust the neckline, alter the hem; make whatever changes are needed. Take the toile apart, alter and then do a final fitting.

5. Take the perfectly-fitting toile apart, lay it on your fabric and cut out.

The other advantage to making a toile is that you are now thoroughly familiar with the pattern and make-up of the garment. This will give you tremendous confidence when cutting out the main fabric and greater speed when constructing.

MEASURING GUIDELINES

1. *Bust* Measure around the fullest part of the bust, using the bra strap as a guide. Be careful not to drop the measure at the back.

If making a fitted top or dress with a bust dart it is important that the bust point finishes in the correct place. You will therefore need to know where the bust point falls from below the shoulder, and the distance from the centre front.

2. *Waist* Take a length of narrow elastic and tie this around your waist. It will naturally sit in the most comfortable place, enabling you to find your true waistline. Now measure.

3. *Hips* Some people are quite curved, unlike the darts you see on commercial patterns. For example, my hips finish approximately 12.5cm (5in) below my waist. If I make a dart 18cm (7in) long, 5cm (2in) will be riding up. The width of the garment will be trying to find a comfortable place to sit. So when I transfer a dart position to a toile, I change it to look like line A (*fig.2*).

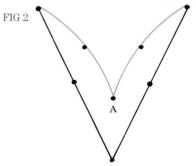

FIG 2

Take the following measurements from the waist down to get an accurate picture of your curve: 5cm (2in), 10cm (4in), 15cm (6in), 20.5cm (8in) and 25cm (10in). At this point you should have reached the fullest part, if not, take further measurements.

4. *Back – Nape of neck to the waist* If you bend your head forward you will find the start point easily by the prominent bone. Measure from this bone to bustline (e.g. bra strap) then down to the waist. Take note of both measurements as alterations can be needed above and below the bustline.

5. *Front* Measure from the shoulder, over the bust point to the waistline, taking two measurements as in point 4. Keep in mind the style of neckline.

6. *Shoulders* Measure a) from shoulder point across the fullest part of the shoulder blades to opposite shoulder point and b) shoulder point to neck point; the measurement needed for one shoulder (*fig.3*).

Whatever your shoulder size, if you are inserting shoulder pads in the

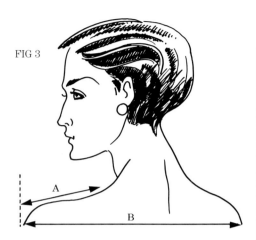

FIG 3

finished garment you must allow for this when fitting the toile.

7. *Sleeves* From shoulder point (including height of shoulder pad) through to elbow down to outer wrist bone. Measure with the arm bent slightly forward, that is, the natural position of the arm. If you measure a perfectly straight arm the sleeves will be too short when relaxed.

8. *Upper Arm* Measure around the fullest part by raising the arm, placing the tape under the top of the arm and then relaxing.

9. *Skirt Length* Try to keep in mind the shoe heel size you will wear with the garment when measuring.

All these measurements will serve as a guideline. Any other problem areas will show up on the toile, providing you have made it up to a reasonable likeness of the finished garment.

RECOMMENDED NOTIONS

Appliqué/Buttonholes I have used Bondaweb (Wonder Under/Vliesofix) for all appliqué work and the bound buttonhole technique. It is a soft, adhesive web, attached to a special paper which can be cut to any shape or size; it is not an interfacing. It will bond one fabric to another through the use of heat from a domestic iron.

Belt Backing I find that Dura-bac (Dura-bac Permafuse) gives a firm, wrinkle-free waistband without any visible ridges and a perfect, even width all round. Dura-bac belting has a 100% cotton base with a polypropylene insert and can be washed or dry cleaned.

Boning Rigilene Boning is widely

available and can be machined in place. For garments in this book I use a 13mm (½in) width for support in the boned bodice, collars and cuffs. Usually available in black or white.

Buttons To cover buttons with thick fabric I recommend a metal base type; the metal claws anchor the fabric securely. For finer fabrics, such as silk crepe de chine, use a plastic base button cover (such as those available from Newey/Dritz) to give a much smoother, rounder appearance.

Elastic Threader Use to thread elastic into a casing without twisting (e.g. Newey Elastic Threader or Dritz Elastic Guide).

Hooks, Eyes and Bars All are made in metal and available in black or silver finish. Cover them using the Couture Technique on page 112. Use a bar instead of an eye when the fastening is laid flat or edge-to-edge with no give.

Horsehair Braid Today it is normally made of nylon and is bias woven. Use it to stiffen and support the hemline. It was often used in the dancing dresses of the 1950's.

Iron and Ironing Board Essential equipment used at every stage of dressmaking. Believe it or not, you can achieve better results simply by your pressing method. Be sure to read my 3-Point Press technique on page 108!

Lead Weights Used to help the drape or fall of a garment. Usually found as individual coin shapes or in long, covered strips. Often used for weighting curtains and can be found in most haberdashery departments.

Loop Turner A wonderful invention for turning through bias strips of fabric. With this tool you can make finished loops as small as 3mm (⅛in) wide. (For example, Newey Rouleau Loop Turner or Dritz Loop Turner.)

Measuring Tools Dressmakers' tape measure and a firm ruler for hems.

Needles – Hand Sewing Betweens or Quilting Betweens are short for quick, even stitching, one stitch at a time. Used by tailors and professional sewers.

Straw or Millinery Needles are long with round eyes; especially suitable for

tacking/basting. They were traditionally used by milliners for work on straw hats and bonnets, hence the name.

Needles – Machine Sewing Always refer to your machine manual for guidance on needle sizes, depending on the type of fabric and thickness of layers you are sewing. Change your needles frequently for best results.

Pins I recommend always using extra long, extra fine pins.

Piping Cord Available in polyester or cotton. The latter is softer but do wash before use to allow for shrinkage.

Press Studs or Sew-On Snaps Use the metal variety and cover with self fabric, following the Couture Technique (page 112). The larger the stud or snap, the greater the hold.

Satin Bias Tape Either purchase or make your own. I have used it to encase the boning in the boned bodice and for finishing hems. Satin is chosen because it is smooth next to the skin and will not stick to stockings.

Scissors Large dressmaking scissors for cutting out and a pair of small scissors for buttonholes and appliqué work.

Shoulder Pads Using the Couture Technique, all shoulder pads will be individually made. However, you will need a plain, uncovered sponge pad (medium set-in shape) as a firm foundation.

Threads EMBROIDERY THREADS Refer to the notions list for applicable designs. POLYESTER General all-round thread, suitable for machine and hand stitching. GÜTERMANN SILK A natural thread of good strength. KINKAME Very fine, pure silk thread, beautiful for machining fine fabrics and hand stitching. Unlikely to knot or tangle in use.

Underarm Dress Shields Most of the garments in this book are really only suitable for dry cleaning. This can be expensive. Use underarm shields which can be removed and washed frequently.

Wadding/Batting Used for quilting or padding out sleeve heads and shoulder pads. Do not use anything above a 56gm (2oz) weight.

Zips All zips used are basic, metal zips.

LA DOLCE VITA DAY DRESS

DESIGN NO. 1

*T*his is a dress which has been designed for the lady who wants to stand out from the crowd and make heads turn.

I decided that if the cut were simple, the detail could afford to be rich, and that meant chic, designer fabrics. Before I even entered the store I knew exactly what I was looking for and could visualize every piece in my mind. I took along my sketch design and before long Mr Joel (the store owner) and I had selected the perfect combination of fabrics and colours. We chose a plain white Duchesse satin from Chanel with an unusual striped flock; heavy black lace for appliqué; a splash of vivid red Duchesse satin and a black and white striped satin. I beamed with delight as my purchases were wrapped. It happens every time and yet the huge pleasure to be derived from selecting fabrics never ceases to amaze me!

Despite my eagerness, it was some time before I had opportunity to make up this design. As I opened up the packages however, the colour and richness of the fabrics brought to mind a setting for the dress; the boldness of monochrome with a dash of eye-catching red set against a sun-soaked piazza. But such an extrovert lady would never be alone; complete the picture with two Dalmatians – the perfect escort!

MATERIALS REQUIRED (SIZES 10–14)

Extra fabric may be required for sizes 12 and 14 if you work with narrower fabrics.
Main fabric: 3m ((3¼yds) flocked Duchesse satin 140cm (52–54in) wide
Interlining: 1.80m (2yds) Bishop's lawn 90cm (35–36in) wide
Skirt Interlining: 3m (3¼yds) stiff net 137cm (54in) wide
Lining: 3.40m (3¾yds) Poult lining 90cm (35–36in) wide
20cm (¼yd) Vilene's Volume Fleece 280 (Pellon Fleece) to pad out shoulders

APPLIQUÉ

30cm (⅓yd) black and white striped satin 109cm (44in) wide
3m (3¼yds) black spotted net 40cm (16in) or wider
1m (1⅛yds) black heavy lace 54cm (21in) wide
10cm (4in) strip of red Duchesse satin
Strip of domette
Iron-on adhesive interleaf, such as Bondaweb/Wonder Under/Vliesofix

METHODS AND TECHNIQUES
INTERLININGS AND THE REASONS WHY
BACK TO FRONT BUTTONHOLES
DARTS
MIXED APPLIQUÉ
LINING PLACEMENT
BELT CARRIERS
SHOULDER PADDING FOR CAP SLEEVES

(RIGHT) I've chosen this colour combination because it turns a simple pattern into a striking design. Alternatively, pastel shades would make a lovely summer cocktail dress.

NOTIONS
Covered belt
5 covered buttons 3cm (1¼in) diameter
5 plain buttons 15mm (⅝in) diameter

PATTERN PIECES
1 Bodice Front, 2 Bodice Back, 3 Front Neck Facing, 4 Skirt, 5 Bodice Front Lining, 6 Bodice Back Lining.
Bodice: Cut 1, 2 and 3 in main fabric and interlining. Cut 5 and 6 in lining fabric.
Skirt: Cut in main fabric, interlining and lining.

THE FABRICS
Main fabric The fabric I used for this dress is an extra special find. It is a Duchesse satin with a flocked, striped design on top. However, a plain Duchesse satin or any rich, special occasion-wear fabric, such as grosgrain or brocade, will do the job just as well.
Interlining Bishop's lawn is a cotton layer used as the interlining for the bodice. It is a very firm, closely woven cotton with lots of body, which will give shape to the bodice.
Stiff Net A very firm net with good sculpturing qualities. It will mould the skirt beautifully and add lots of body to hold the many pleats in shape.
Lining Poult; a good, firm lining to maintain the shape of this dress.

METHOD
BODICE
1. You will need all three pattern pieces in main fabric and lawn. Lay the lawn to the wrong side of the main fabric and

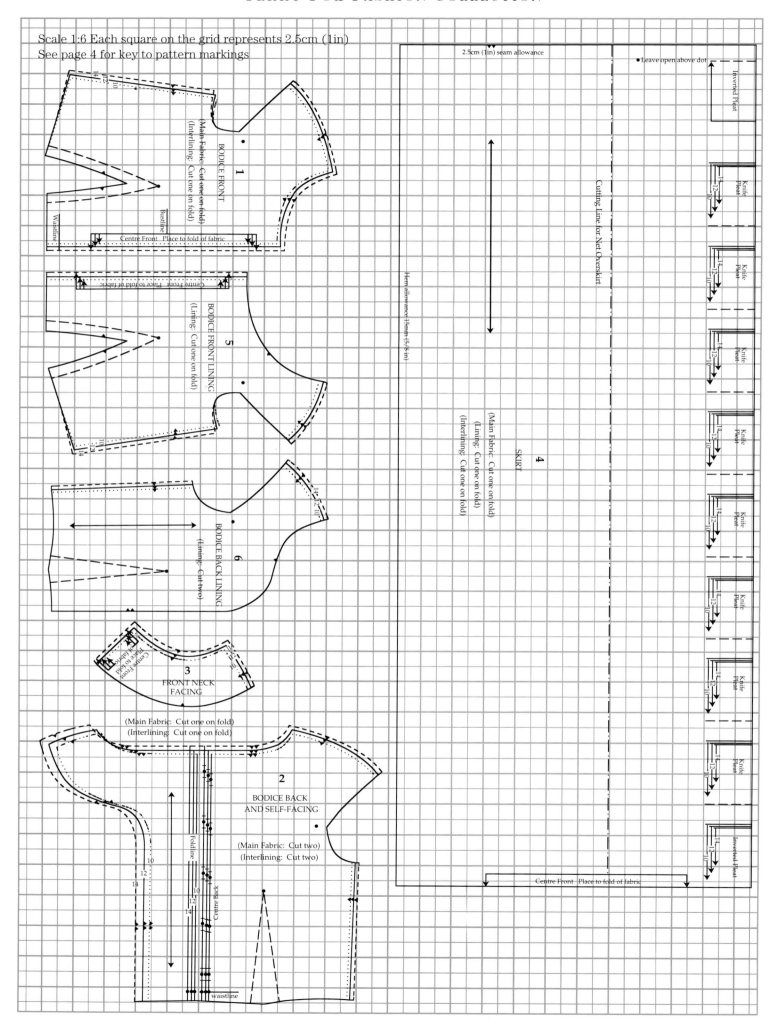

Scale 1:6 Each square on the grid represents 2.5cm (1in)
See page 4 for key to pattern markings

2.5cm (1in) seam allowance

• Leave open above dot

Inverted Pleat

Cutting Line for Net Overskirt

Hem allowance 15mm (5/8 in)

1
BODICE FRONT
(Main Fabric: Cut one on fold)
(Interlining: Cut one on fold)
Waistline
Bustline
Centre Front   Place to fold of fabric

5
BODICE FRONT LINING
(Lining: Cut one on fold)
Centre Front Place to fold of fabric

6
BODICE BACK LINING
(Lining: Cut two)

3
FRONT NECK
FACING
Centre Front Place to fold
(Main Fabric: Cut one on fold)
(Interlining: Cut one on fold)

2
BODICE BACK
AND SELF-FACING
(Main Fabric: Cut two)
(Interlining: Cut two)
Foldline
Centre Back
waistline

4
SKIRT
(Main Fabric: Cut one on fold)
(Lining: Cut one on fold)
(Interlining: Cut one on fold)
Centre Front   Place to fold of fabric

Knife Pleat
Knife Pleat
Knife Pleat
Knife Pleat
Knife Pleat
Knife Pleat
Knife Pleat
Inverted Pleat

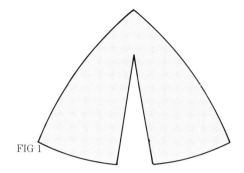
FIG 1

press together. Blindstitch the lawn to the main fabric along the Centre Back foldline on left and right bodice Back. Tack all around the outer edges so the two layers work as one.

2. Make the darts (page 112, Couture Techniques) in the front and back and press towards the centre.

3. Join the bodice Back to the Front at the shoulder and side seams. Join facings at shoulder seams. Clip if necessary and press open.

4. Place the bodice facing to the neck edge, right sides together, matching shoulder seams, Centre Fronts and Centre Backs. Pin and machine a 15mm ($^5/_8$in) seam allowance. Layer the seam, clip and turn to the right side. Press lightly, making sure the neck seam is slightly towards the inside of the garment. Press lightly down the Centre Back foldlines.

5. Staystitch 13mm ($^1/_2$in) from the raw edge of the armhole and clip up to the stitching line.

6. Cut a triangle of Volume Fleece to fit into the cap sleeve, for a slightly padded effect. Cut through the fleece at the shoulder seam and overlap it to accommodate the curve of the shoulder (*fig. 1*). Overstitch the overlap and then overstitch the fleece to the lawn layer only, around the outer edge (*fig.2*).

Repeat for the other shoulder. Now turn back the clipped armhole seam and overstitch to the lawn and fleece round both armholes (*fig.3*).

7. Next machine all bodice lining pieces together. Stitch darts. Press and clip where necessary.

8. Place lining to facing (right sides together), clipping where necessary to ease. Pin in place. Now machine a 15mm ($^5/_8$in) seam allowance, starting at the waist, up through the Centre Back and Back facing to the Front facing and down the other side. Turn the lining through to the right side and press. The seam should be pressed towards the lining.

9. Clip around the armhole lining and turn the 15mm ($^5/_8$in) allowance to the wrong side. Pin the lining to the dress around the armhole. Using a tiny stitch,

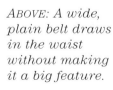
ABOVE: A wide, plain belt draws in the waist without making it a big feature.

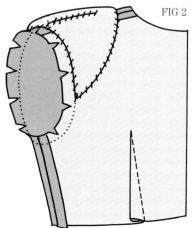
FIG 2

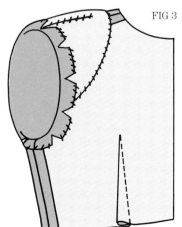
FIG 3

15

LEFT: Add extra fullness to the skirt with a three-layered black net petticoat.

slipstitch in place and repeat for the other armhole.

10. Secure the facing along the neck edge, prickstitching through to the interlining only.

SKIRT

You will need the skirt pieces in main fabric, net and lining; all cut the same.

Now prepare the fabric needed for the appliqué and skirt border.

BORDER APPLIQUÉ

1. Cut pieces of striped fabric in varying squares and rectangles, bearing in mind the border that I created is 35cm (14in) deep. Turn in the raw edges of the pieces and press lightly.

2. Lay the main fabric of the skirt out flat on a level surface, with right side uppermost. Place the shapes to the bottom edge of the skirt fabric, positioning them horizontally and vertically. Pin them right side uppermost and then slipstitch in place. If the edge of a square or rectangle is to lie at the bottom edge of the skirt do not turn under the raw edge since it will be machined under later (*fig. 4*).

3. Now cut a length of spotted net, two-thirds the depth of the skirt but the same width as the skirt, as it is laid out.

Lay the net on top of the skirt (right

FIG 4

side uppermost), lining up the bottom edge of the net with the lower skirt edge. The striped pieces should now all be covered. Secure the net by tacking around both sides and the lower edge. Secure the top edge with pins only.

4. Cut a length of black lace to go the full width of the skirt (width A to B on *fig. 4*). The lace I used was a very heavy, open lace, 54cm (21in) wide. However, the design of the lace allowed me to divide it into three lengths, each approximately 18cm (7in) wide, so I joined three lengths of lace to go all the way round the skirt.

Lay the lace on top of the spotted net, right side facing you, taking care to conceal any joins you may have to make in the lace. Pin in place so that the top edge of the lace is just inside the top edge of the net. Now machine in place. I used a straight stitch on this heavy lace, but a finer lace, perhaps cut from an all-over lace design, could be secured with a small zigzag stitch. Refer to the Appliqué section dealing with lace (Couture Techniques) for guidance.

5. Stitch the lace along the top edge, following the line of your lace pattern, down the Centre Back, along the bottom edge and back to your starting point. Make sure the lace pattern will match when joined at the Centre Back,

Leaf template, actual size

bearing in mind that a seam allowance will be taken out later. Trim away any of the spotted net which extends beyond the top of the lace.

6. Now turn to the remaining scraps of lace and the red satin. I found an extra five flowers in my lace and cut them out individually. I then cut the same shape in red satin, but slightly smaller than the lace. I placed the red satin pieces evenly around the skirt, just above the lace strip, starting with one shape at the Centre Front. Pin each flower on top, keeping the red satin underneath.

7. Using the leaf template provided (above), cut out five leaves in red satin and domette. Follow the Padded Appliqué method in the Couture Techniques section, page 108, to complete each leaf.

8. Now position the leaves underneath each red satin and black lace flower that you have already pinned onto the dress. Place them so that they peep out from under the flower. When satisfied with the placement, peel off the Bondaweb backing and fuse the leaves in place.

Using a small, close zigzag stitch, fix the leaves securely in place. The Appliqué technique on page 108 will give you guidance. You will have to move the red and black flowers while you do this.

Now replace the red and black flowers in position and using the same method, machine them in place to complete the appliqué work.

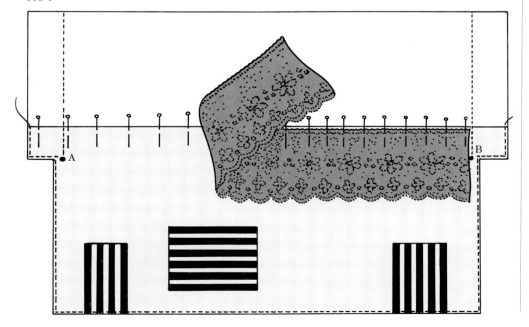

RIGHT: This black lace has clearly defined flower and leaf motifs. Use the pattern from your own lace to make alternative shapes.

BELOW: Lovely, big covered buttons in keeping with the bold style of this dress do not need wide buttonholes when you use the back to front buttonhole technique.

the markings transferred from the paper pattern for position and direction. Pin and tack in place.

15. Bring the skirt to the bodice, right sides together and matching up Centre Front, Back and side notches. Machine the two together at the waistline but do not stitch the bodice lining. This will be hand secured later to cover the seam allowance.

Turn in the facing at the Centre Back and then turn under the bottom edge seam allowance of the bodice lining. Slipstitch this in place.

FINISHING TOUCHES

The dress is finished with a 7.5cm (3in) wide, professionally covered belt. You may wish to add two belt carriers, positioned at the side seams, to hold the belt in place.

1. Cut a strip of main fabric 2.5cm (1in) wide, 18cm (7in) long. Try to incorporate the selvedge in the length. Turn under 8mm (⅓in) on the long raw edge. Now overlap it with the selvedge and press. You should now have a strip measuring approximately 8mm (⅓in) × 18cm (7in).

2. Edgestitch along the two long sides.

3. Cut the strip in half to form the two belt carriers, each approximately 8mm (⅓in) × 9cm (3½in).

4. Turn in 6mm (¼in) at each raw end. Hand overstitch the carriers to the skirt at the waistline by laying each vertically along the side seam, up to the bodice.

Now complete the Centre Back fastening with Back to Front Buttonholes (see Couture Techniques for step-by-step guidance).

5. Position the five large covered buttons on the left bodice Back, along the Centre Back seam. Hand stitch in place through to the facing.

6. On the inside stitch five smaller buttons to the left facing, using the stitch marks from the outer large buttons for positioning. The corresponding small buttonholes should then be made on the right Back bodice.

Thread the belt through the carriers and your outfit is complete – and guaranteed to dazzle on any occasion!

SKIRT CONSTRUCTION CONTINUED

9. Machine the Centre Back seam of the skirt from the small • down to the skirt edge. Clip up to the • to allow you to press the seam flat open.

10. Lay the skirt net for the interlining to the wrong side of the satin skirt, overlapping the seam allowances at the Centre Back seam. Tack around the waistline and hemline. Use a permanent hand stitch to secure the net to the seam allowance at Centre Back. Turn skirt to the right side.

11. With the back of the skirt facing you, press the Left Centre Back to the wrong side along the seamline. Press under 13mm (½in) on the Right Centre Back in order to form a 13mm (½in) underlap.

12. Prepare the Centre Back seam of the skirt lining as you did the main fabric; press seam open. With right sides together, place the lining to the main skirt at hem level. Matching up Centre Back, Centre Front and sides, pin in place. Machine, taking the full 15mm (⅝in) seam allowance. Layer the seams and press.

Now turn the lining through to the right side and take it up to the waistline. Press the hemline very firmly, ensuring that the seamline lies ever so slightly to the wrong side.

13. Tack the lining to the main skirt at the waistline. Turn under the lining at the Centre Back opening and slipstitch in place.

14. Make the pleats at the waist, using

PINK APPLIQUÉD SUIT

The appliqué design of this suit was inspired by a birthday card I received which depicted a vase of flowers. I like playing with assortments of materials and laces to decorate a plain fabric; it gives me the sense that I am creating not just the garment but the fabric too. Many people craft their appliqué ideas into cushions and wall-hangings but I like to see people wearing and enjoying their 'special creations'.

I carried the appliqué idea in the back of my mind for several months until I discovered a superb collection of designer silks. The pink silk, used as the main fabric, was equally interesting on both sides which made it ideal for this suit with contrasting lapels. Then I found the grosgrain, a tiny stripe in two shades, perfect for the double binding. These fabrics soon took shape as the frame for my picture of cream and pink lace flowers, subtle pink satin roses, lace leaves and striped vase. The dramatic cut of the suit prevents the suit from appearing too dainty but combines with the delicate appliqué to provide a little feminine sex appeal, don't you think?

MATERIALS REQUIRED

Main fabric size 10: 3.90m (4 ¼yds) shantung 115cm (44–45in) wide; size 12: 4m (4⅓yds); size 14: 4.20m (4½yds).

Interlining size 10: 3.50m (3⅞yds) firm cotton mull 115cm (44–45in) wide; size 12: 3.60m (4yds); size 14: 3.70m (4⅛yds).

Interlining No 2 size 10: 50cm (⅔yd) firm collar and cuff canvas 93cm (37in) wide; size 12: 60cm (⅔yd); size 14: 60cm (⅔yd).

Interlining No 3 size 10: 50cm (⅔yd) domette 90cm (35-36in) wide; size 12: 60cm (⅔yd); size 14: 60cm (⅔yd).

Interfacing size 10: 1.60m (1¾yds) white duck linen 60cm (24in) wide; size 12: 1.60m (1¾yds); size 14: 1.70m (1⅞yds).

Lining size 10: 2.90m (3⅛yds) Habutai silk 90cm (35–36in) wide; size 12: 2.90m (3⅛yds); size 14: 2.90m (3⅛yds).

Double-Edge bindings – wide width and facings size 10: 1.80m (2yds) grosgrain 115cm (44–45in) wide; size 12: 1.90m (2yds); size 14: 2m (2⅛yds).

Narrow width bindings size 10: 90cm (1yd) grosgrain 115cm (44–45in) wide; size 12: 1m (1⅛yds); size 14: 1m (1⅛yds).

NOTIONS

One pair medium sponge set-in shoulder pads

LEFT: A design for the theatrical and not so shy. It could be toned down by leaving off the collar and cuffs altogether.

Small piece lightweight wadding/batting
25cm (10in) boning
18cm (7in) skirt zip
Belt backing 2.5cm (1in) wide cut to waist size
4 large covered buttons 3.2cm (1¼in) diameter
3 neutral-coloured buttons 2.5cm (1in) diameter (used inside the jacket)

METHODS AND TECHNIQUES
Jacket
INTERLININGS AND THE REASONS WHY
COLLAR AND REVERS WITH EXTRA LONG POINTS
BONED CUFF
SHOULDER PADS AND SLEEVE HEADS
DARTS
LINING
BACK TO FRONT BUTTONHOLES
DOUBLE-EDGE BINDINGS
APPLIQUÉ
COVERED HOOK AND BAR

Skirt
INTERLININGS
WAISTBAND
HANGING LOOPS
ZIP
LINING WITH BACK VENT
DOUBLE-EDGE BINDINGS

APPLIQUÉ

Lace in various shapes and colours
Plain silk scraps
(I used the reverse of the main fabric and grosgrain)
Domette for padding the appliqué
Bondaweb/Wonder Under/Vliesofix

PATTERN PIECES

Jacket: 1 Front, 2 Back, 3 Sleeve, 4 Collar, 5 Revers, 6 Cuff, 7 Front Facing, 8 Back Neck Facing, 9 Back Hem Facing, 10 Front Hem Facing, 11 Sleeve Hem Facing, 12 Front Interfacing, 13 Back Interfacing, 14 Interfacing Front Hem, 15 Interfacing Back Hem, 16 Front Lining, 17 Back Lining, 28 Appliqué Vase Template.

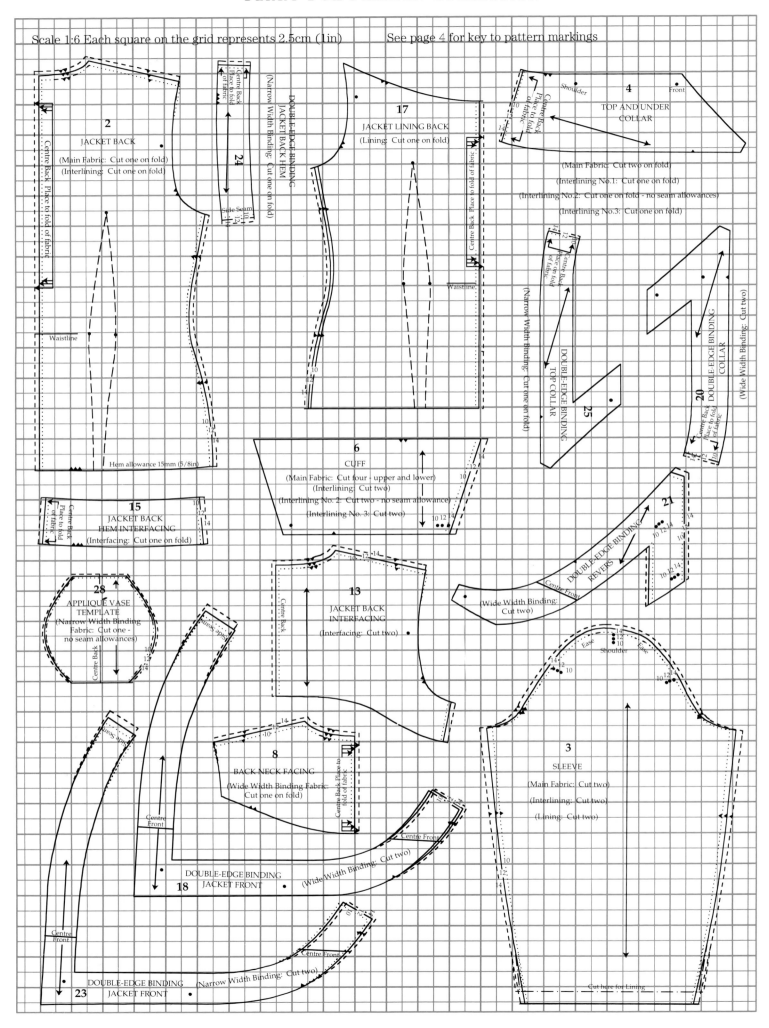

Scale 1:6 Each square on the grid represents 2.5cm (1in)   See page 4 for key to pattern markings

2 JACKET BACK
(Main Fabric: Cut one on fold)
(Interlining: Cut one on fold)
Centre Back Place to fold of fabric
Waistline
Hem allowance 15mm (5/8in)

DOUBLE-EDGE BINDING JACKET BACK HEM
(Narrow Width Binding: Cut one on fold)
24
Side Seam

17 JACKET LINING BACK
(Lining: Cut one on fold)
Centre Back Place to fold of fabric
Waistline

4 TOP AND UNDER COLLAR
Shoulder   Front
Centre Back Place to fold of fabric
(Main Fabric: Cut two on fold)
(Interlining No.1: Cut one on fold)
(Interlining No.2: Cut one on fold - no seam allowances)
(Interlining No.3: Cut one on fold)

DOUBLE-EDGE BINDING TOP COLLAR
(Narrow Width Binding: Cut one on fold)
25
Centre Back place on fold of fabric

DOUBLE-EDGE BINDING COLLAR
(Wide Width Binding: Cut two)
20
Centre Back place to fold of fabric

15 JACKET BACK HEM INTERFACING
(Interfacing: Cut one on fold)
Centre Back Place to fold of fabric

6 CUFF
(Main Fabric: Cut four - upper and lower)
(Interlining: Cut two)
(Interlining No. 2: Cut two - no seam allowance)
(Interlining No. 3: Cut two)

DOUBLE-EDGE BINDING REVERS
(Wide Width Binding: Cut two)
21

28 APPLIQUÉ VASE TEMPLATE
(Narrow Width Binding Fabric: Cut one - no seam allowances)
Centre Back

13 JACKET BACK INTERFACING
(Interfacing: Cut two)
Centre Back

3 SLEEVE
(Main Fabric: Cut two)
(Interlining: Cut two)
(Lining: Cut two)
Ease   Shoulder   Ease
Cut here for Lining

8 BACK NECK FACING
(Wide Width Binding Fabric: Cut one on fold)
Centre Back Place to fold of fabric

DOUBLE-EDGE BINDING JACKET FRONT
18
(Wide Width Binding: Cut two)
Centre Front

DOUBLE-EDGE BINDING JACKET FRONT
23
(Narrow Width Binding: Cut two)
Centre Front

Scale 1:6 Each square on the grid represents 2.5cm (1in)   See page 4 for key to pattern markings

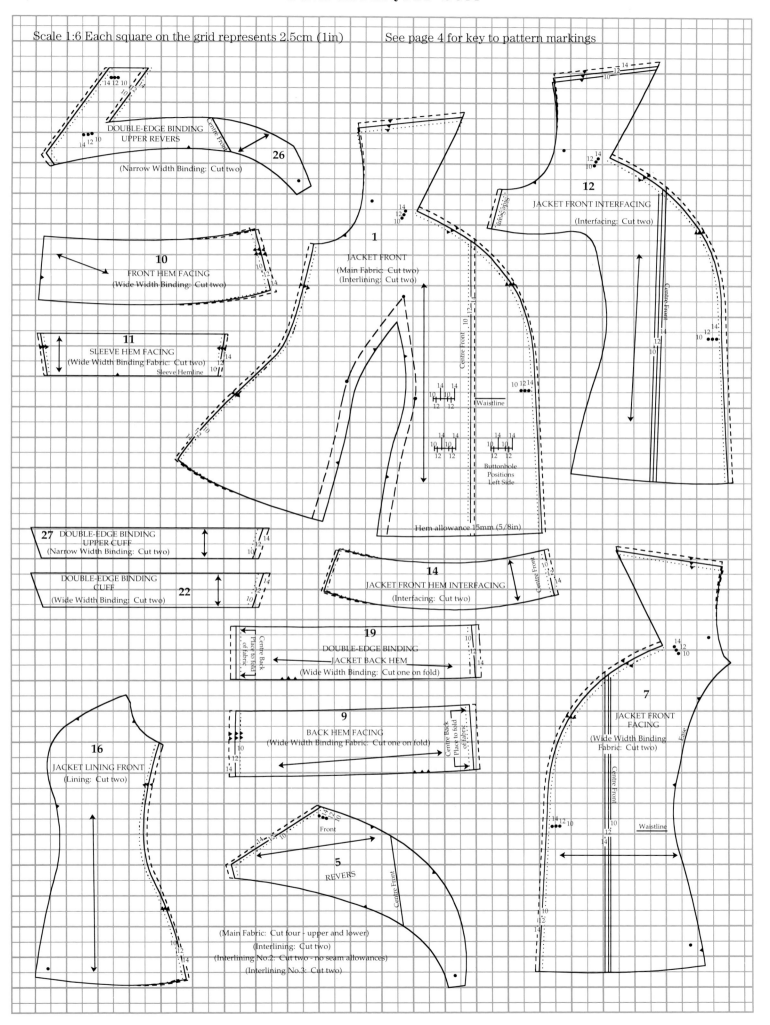

DOUBLE-EDGE BINDING
UPPER REVERS

(Narrow Width Binding: Cut two)

26

10
FRONT HEM FACING
(Wide Width Binding: Cut two)

11
SLEEVE HEM FACING
(Wide Width Binding Fabric: Cut two)
Sleeve Hemline

1
JACKET FRONT
(Main Fabric: Cut two)
(Interlining: Cut two)

Centre Front

Waistline

Buttonhole
Positions
Left Side

Hem allowance 15mm (5/8in)

12
JACKET FRONT INTERFACING
(Interfacing: Cut two)

Centre Front

27 DOUBLE-EDGE BINDING
UPPER CUFF
(Narrow Width Binding: Cut two)

DOUBLE-EDGE BINDING
CUFF
(Wide Width Binding: Cut two)   **22**

14
JACKET FRONT HEM INTERFACING
(Interfacing: Cut two)

Centre Front

19
DOUBLE-EDGE BINDING
JACKET BACK HEM
(Wide Width Binding: Cut one on fold)
Centre Back
Place to fold
of fabric

9
BACK HEM FACING
(Wide Width Binding Fabric: Cut one on fold)
Centre Back
Place to fold of fabric

7
JACKET FRONT
FACING
(Wide Width Binding
Fabric: Cut two)
Centre Front

Waistline

16
JACKET LINING FRONT
(Lining: Cut two)

Front

5
REVERS
Centre Front

(Main Fabric: Cut four - upper and lower)
(Interlining: Cut two)
(Interlining No.2: Cut two - no seam allowances)
(Interlining No.3: Cut two)

LEFT: Make a long silk skirt to go with this jacket and you will create a dramatic evening outfit.

Skirt: 1 Front, 2 Back, 3 Waistband, 4 Front Hem Facing, 5 Back Hem Facing.

Double-Edge Binding
Jacket: Wide Bindings: 18 Front, 19 Back Hem, 20 Collar, 21 Revers, 22 Cuff.
Narrow Bindings: 23 Front, 24 Back Hem, 25 Top Collar, 26 Upper Revers, 27 Upper Cuff.
Skirt: Wide Bindings: 6 Front, 7 Back.
Narrow Bindings: 8 Front, 9 Back.

THE FABRICS

Main fabric The light, but firm shantung has a very slight slub and two very different faces; satin finish one side and matt on the other. The satin side looks slightly lighter in colour due to the sheen. I have used the matt side for the main part of the jacket and skirt; the satin side for cuffs, collars and revers.

Interlining Although the main fabric is firm, it will not hold the jacket shape and prevent seating in the skirt. The firm mull will hold the shape, adding the extra strength plus the density required for the light pink of the main fabric.

Interfacing Duck linen, very crisp and firm, this will add a wonderful support to the interfaced areas of the jacket. The hemline is also interfaced to prevent the peplum effect collapsing.

Lining The jacket is a light, fitted garment; designed to be worn as a top, not over a blouse. A lightweight Habutai silk lining will be cool and comfortable to wear close to the skin, without adding extra bulk, which is important, particularly in the skirt.

METHOD

JACKET

1. Cut the following pieces:
Main fabric: 1, 2, 3, 4, 5, and 6
Interlining: 1, 2, 3, 4, 5, 6
Interlining No 2: 4, 5, 6
Interlining No 3: 4, 5, 6
Interfacing: 12, 13, 14, 15

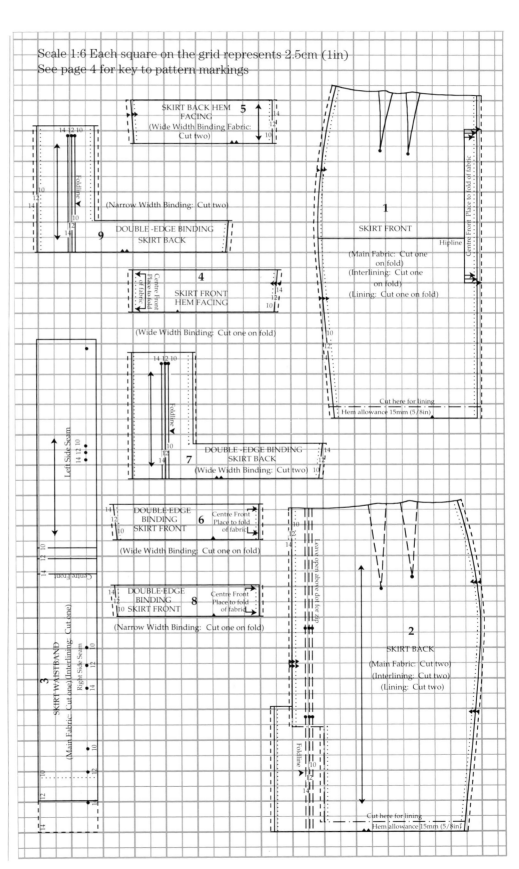

Scale 1:6 Each square on the grid represents 2.5cm (1in)
See page 4 for key to pattern markings

See Couture Techniques page 108 for all appliqué methods. All shapes actual size. Apply to garment in the following sequence.

VASE (see page 22 for pattern piece): cut one in pink grosgrain and apply, using Fabric Appliqué method.

1. Lace leaf: cut three. Lace Appliqué method.

2. Satin flower: cut three using main fabric reversed. Padded Appliqué method.

3. Satin flower (small): cut two and apply using above method.

4. Large cream flower: cut one full size and one half size in lace; cut one and a half, slightly smaller, in a contrasting colour (e.g. pink). See technique for Adding Colour.

5. Large pink lace flower: cut five and apply direct to jacket Back. Lace Appliqué method.

6. Medium pink lace flower: cut three, method as above.

7. Small pink lace flower: cut one, work as above.

8. Small cream lace flower: cut two, apply as above.

Use this design as a guide: your lace and colours may differ.

The appliqué and double-edge binding techniques are not restricted to this suit. Use them on any suitable garment or even around the home for exclusive interior decor!

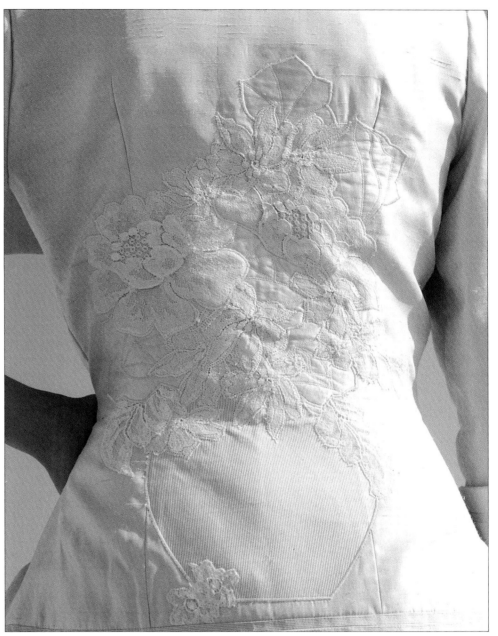

Lining: 3, 16, 17

Grey Double-Edge Binding (wide width): 7, 8, 9, 10, 11, 18, 19, 20, 21, 22

Pink Double-Edge Binding (narrow width): 23, 24, 25, 26, 27, 28

2. Take the main fabric and mull pattern pieces 1, 2 and 3. Mount the mull to the corresponding silk pieces by pressing first, then tack together and treat as one.

3. Machine the darts in back and front (Couture Techniques page 112).

4. Following the chart and instructions for the appliqué method, complete the design on the jacket Back. The large fabric flowers are padded with domette. The large lace flowers have a slightly different shade of pink satin placed underneath to give contrast.

5. Now take the interfacing pieces 12 (Front) and 13 (Back). Trim the Centre Back seam of the linen to 6mm (¼in), overlap and cross stitch together.

6. Position the Back interfacing to the wrong side of the jacket Back. Pin the Front interfacing to the wrong side of the jacket Front, tacking all the way round the outer edge to secure. Use a herringbone stitch to permanently fix

BELOW: Key to appliqué pieces

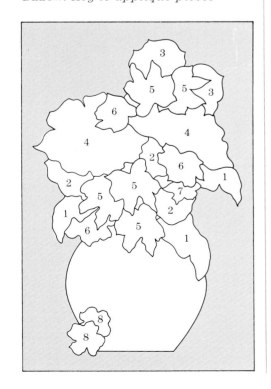

the inside edge of the interfacing to the interlining.

7. Machine Fronts to Back at shoulder seams and side seams. Clip and press open seams.

8. Machine side seams of sleeves. Clip and press open. Set in the sleeves and sleeve heads following the Couture Techniques. Cover the sponge shoulder pads following instructions on page 119.

9. Place interfacing pieces 14 and 15 to the wrong side of the hemline. Trim to

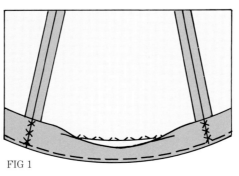

FIG 1

6mm (¼in) from the side seams; overlap the edges and cross stitch.

10. Tack along the bottom edge and blindstitch the top edge by rolling back the interfacing slightly and stitching between the linen and mull only (*fig.1*).

11. *Double-Edge Binding* Use the Couture Technique on page 113 to double bind the Top collar, one pair of revers, one pair of cuffs, jacket front and hemline.

12. Make up the deep pointed collar and revers by following the instructions on page 112. Use the cotton mull as the cotton interlining. Place the finished Top collar to the Under collar on the right side of the jacket. Match up Front •, shoulder • and Centre Back. Tack in place at neck edge.

13. Place bound revers to Front neck edge, with right sides uppermost and matching •s. Tack in place (*fig.2*).

RIGHT: The double binding is one of my favourite finishes – it gives an immediate designer look. Add fine silks to thick wools or vice versa. The perfect background would be an edge-to-edge Chanel suit.

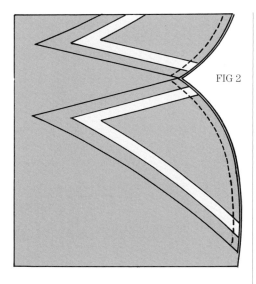

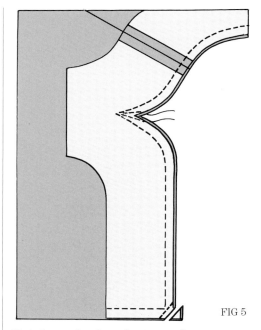

FIG 2

14. Construct the boned cuffs, again using Couture Techniques, page 110. Use the cotton mull as the cotton interlining layer.

15. Place cuffs to the bottom of the sleeve, Under cuff against the right side of the fabric, matching up side seams. Machine, taking a 13mm ($\frac{1}{2}$in) seam allowance. Clip as necessary up to the machine line (*fig.3*). Now turn 15mm ($\frac{5}{8}$in) to the inside of the sleeve and overstitch this to the sleeve interlining (*fig.4*).

the Centre Backs (top and bottom), neck edge, shoulder seams, front neckline, front edge, hemline and side seams. Pin in place then machine around the entire outer edge, taking the full 15mm ($\frac{5}{8}$in) seam allowance. Reinforce the neck edge corners where the collar meets the revers, clip (*fig.5*).

───────── TIP ─────────

Machine an extra row of stitches across the corners immediately outside the original stitching line. Reverse at the corner by about three stitches and then machine forward again. This will reinforce the corner and will enable you to eliminate the bulk completely when trimming.

FIG 5

Reinforce the front bottom edge corners of the jacket. Layer all seams, clipping where necessary.

18. Turn the facing through and press flat. Prickstitch the facing all the way round, stitching through to the interlining only.

19. *Lining* Machine darts in Front and Back. Join the Fronts to the Back at the side seams. Clip and press seams open, pressing darts towards the centre.

20. With right sides together, place the lining inside the jacket and pin. Machine stitch the Back and Front lining to the Back and Front facings respectively. Stop at the lower notch on the Front facing. Press the seam allowance towards the lining.

21. Join the side seams of the sleeve lining; join sleeve facing seam. Press the seams. With right sides together machine the facing to the bottom edge of the sleeve lining. Press the seam towards the lining.

22. Clip up the hem of the sleeve facing to 13mm ($\frac{1}{2}$in), then turn under 15mm ($\frac{5}{8}$in) and press.

23. Set the sleeve lining into each armhole; clip and press.

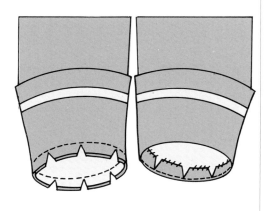

FIG 3   FIG 4

16. *Facings* Join the Back and Front facing at the shoulder seams. Join the Back and Front hem facings at the side seam, and then join to the Front facing. Press all seams open.

17. With right sides together lay the facing on top of the jacket, matching up

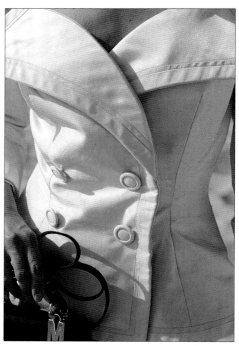

LEFT: Try different patterns for the double binding, separated by a line of piping to coordinate them.

FIG 7

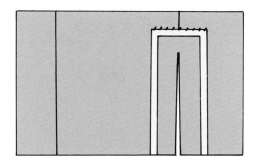

24. Position the shoulder pads and secure in place to the main garment.
25. Bring the sleeve lining down through the main sleeve to the hemline. Matching up the side seams, pin the facing to the bottom of the sleeve (*fig.6*). Use a small slipstitch to catch the facing to the cuff at hemline.

FIG 6

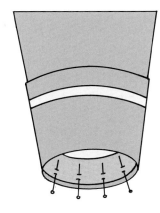

26. Bar tack the shoulder seam to the shoulder pad at the armhole edge.
27. Press under a 15mm (⁵⁄₈in) seam allowance at the hemline of the jacket lining. Lay this to the top of the hem facing, overlapping by 15mm (⁵⁄₈in). Fold the lining down at hem level where it meets the facing. Slipstitch in place.
28. *Buttonholes* Follow the Couture Technique for Back to Front Buttonholes (page 111). Position large, covered buttons on the upper face of the jacket, using the tissue pattern for placement. I have had these buttons professionally covered with a bound edge in two fabrics, to match the double binding.
29. Finally, you will need a covered hook and bar at the Centre Front to prevent the neckline gaping (see Couture Technique page 112).

SKIRT
1. Cut out:
Main Fabric: 1, 2, 3
Interlining: 1, 2, 3
Lining: 1, 2
Grey Double-Edge Binding Fabric (wide width): 4, 5, 6, 7
Pink Double-Edge Binding Fabric (narrow width): 8, 9
2. Mount together 1, 2 and 3 in mull and

main fabric and treat as one layer. Make the darts in Front and Back skirt.
3. Make up the double-edge binding for the hem (pattern pieces 6, 7, 8 and 9) and machine to the hemline of the skirt, using the Double Binding technique on page 113. Note: At the top of the skirt vent (right side of fabric), you will have to turn under the upper edge of the binding by hand and blindstitch (*fig. 7*).
4. Bearing in mind that the Centre Back seam has a 2.5cm (1in) seam allowance, machine the Centre Back between the notches, leaving the opening for the zip. Press open the seam and insert the zip following the Couture Technique.
5. Machine Front to Back at the side seams ensuring the bindings match up. Clip and press seams open.
6. Join the Front hem facing to Back hem facing, then to Centre Back self-facing. Press all seams open.
7. With right sides together place the facing on the hemline, matching up side seams and the Centre Front. Pin then machine the 15mm (⁵⁄₈in) allowance, reinforcing the corners as described earlier (*fig.8*). Turn through to the wrong side and press. Blindstitch all around the facing, securing to the interlining layer only.

FIG 8

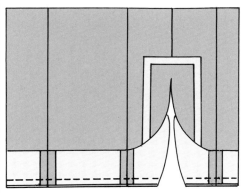

8. *Lining* Machine the darts in Front and Back. Press towards the centre.
9. Machine Front and Back together at the side seams. Clip as necessary and press open seams.
10. With wrong sides together, place the skirt lining inside the main skirt; matching Centre Front, Centre Back and side seams. Pin at the waist.

11. Turn in the raw edge of the lining at the zip opening and slipstitch in place.
12. Make two hanging loops (folded length 25cm /10in) from lining scraps, using the Rouleau Technique on page 116. Secure to the side seams of the skirt, hanging downwards.
13. *Waistband* Machine all the way round the waist 6mm (¹⁄₄in) from the upper raw edge, to keep all the layers level and in one place.
14. Place the waistband and belt backing at the upper edge of the skirt following the Waistband Technique, page 120. Finish the waistband with two covered hooks and bars (see page 112).
15. *Hem* Turn the skirt inside out, with the lining hanging down to the main fabric hemline. Snip into the corners of the lining back vent (*fig.9*). Now turn under 15mm (⁵⁄₈in) all the way round the lining hemline and vent; press. Place the bottom of the lining to the top of the hem, overlapping by 15mm (⁵⁄₈in). Pin in place around the vent and hem and slipstitch (*fig.10*). A natural pleat will form at the bottom edge giving an ease allowance.

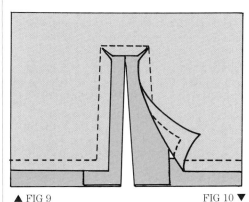

▲ FIG 9   FIG 10 ▼

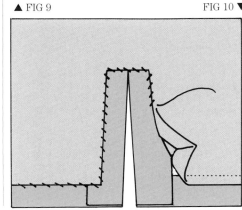

FLORAL SUIT

*T*his suit was born from a creative urge to take the role of interlining layers beyond anything I had ever done before.

I fell in love with the fabric as soon as I saw it. It was very fresh and colourful, very alive and fun. But the fabric type presented an all too common problem. The fabric was perfect in colour and pattern, but totally unsuitable for the garment I had in mind. The soft pure silk crepe de chine I had chosen was very light and floaty to handle; much more suitable for draping in long, softly pleated skirts, dresses and feminine blouses.

But to me the fabric design had a very 1950s feel to it and all I could think of was a short, sharp, summer suit, worn with stiletto shoes and little white gloves. However much I thought about the more suitable styles for the fabric, my suit kept coming back to mind.

What if I could totally control the fabric, by combining the interlinings I had used before on other garments? Excitement rose at the endless possibilities available.

I gathered up all my interlining samples, threw them on the table and started to play. The tailored silk suit was about to be born!

MATERIALS REQUIRED

(Jacket and skirt unless otherwise specified)

Main fabric size 10: 3.10m (3¹/₃yds) lightweight pure silk crepe de chine 115cm (44–45in) wide; size 12: 3.20m (3¹/₂yds); size 14: 3.30m (3²/₃yds).

Interlining No 1 size 10: 3.70m (4¹/₈yds) cotton mull 90cm (36in) wide; size 12: 3.80m (4¹/₄yds); size 14: 3.90m (4¹/₄yds).

Interlining No 2 size 10 (jacket): 1.90m (2yds) Poult lining 90cm (36in) wide; size 12: 1.90m (2yds); size 14: 1.90m (2yds)

Interlining No 3 size 10 (skirt): 60cm (²/₃yd) Bremsilk 140cm (52–54in) wide; size 12: 60cm (²/₃yd); size 14: 60cm (²/₃yds).

Lining size 10: 2.70m (3yds) Habutai silk 90cm (36in) wide; size 12: 2.80m (3¹/₈yds); size 14: 2.90m (3¹/₈yds).

Interfacing No 1 (jacket) size 10: 1.50m (1²/₃yds) Duck linen 60cm (24in) wide; size 12: 1.60m (1³/₄yds); size 14: 1.60m (1³/₄yds).

Interfacing No 2 (jacket) size 10: 30cm (¹/₃yd) Holland linen 81cm (32in) wide; size 12: 30cm (¹/₃yd); size 14: 30cm (¹/₃yd).

Piping cord cover: 45cm (¹/₂yd) each plain silk and lining fabric.

NOTIONS:

1.70m (2yds) piping cord 3mm (¹/₈in) diameter
2 shoulder pads
3 buttons 2.5cm (1in) diameter
18cm (7in) zip
Petersham/waistband ribbon
Medium hook and eye

METHODS AND TECHNIQUES

BUILDING UP OF UNDER LAYERS AND THE
REASONS WHY
SHOULDER PADS
DARTS
COVERED PIPING CORD
BOUND BUTTONHOLES
SETTING-IN SLEEVES
SLEEVE HEADS
LINING AND HEMS
RIBBON WAISTBAND
HANGING LOOPS
ZIP

1m (1¹/₈yds) satin bias tape 2cm (³/₄in) wide

PATTERN PIECES

Jacket: 1 Back, 2 Front, 3 Sleeves, 4 Under Collar, 5 Top Collar, 6 Front Facing, 7 Back Neck Facing, 8 Front Interfacing, 9 Back Interfacing, 10 Revers Interfacing, 11 Front Lining, 12 Back Lining.
Skirt: 1 Front, 2 Back.

THE FABRICS

We need to change the main fabric quite considerably in order for it to act properly in this tailored suit. Obviously the crepe de chine is unsuitable for structuring a jacket of this type, but perfect for a softly pleated or gathered

RIGHT: Study the make-up of this crisply tailored silk suit carefully and you will gain a lifetime's knowledge of couture dressmaking.

Scale 1:6 Each square on the grid represents 2.5cm (1in)   See page 4 for key to pattern markings

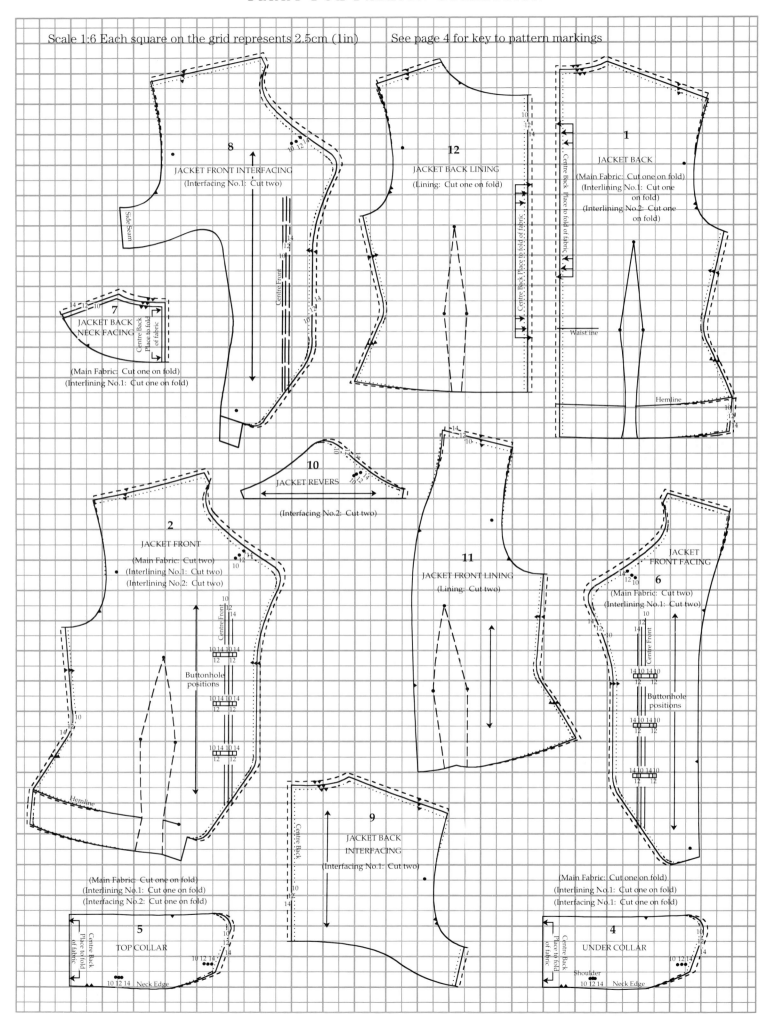

8
JACKET FRONT INTERFACING
(Interfacing No.1: Cut two)

Side Seam

Centre Front

7
JACKET BACK
NECK FACING

Centre Back
Place to fold
of fabric

(Main Fabric: Cut one on fold)
(Interlining No.1: Cut one on fold)

12
JACKET BACK LINING
(Lining: Cut one on fold)

Centre Back Place to fold of fabric

1
JACKET BACK
(Main Fabric: Cut one on fold)
(Interlining No.1: Cut one on fold)
(Interlining No.2: Cut one on fold)

Centre Back Place to fold of fabric

Waistline

Hemline

10
JACKET REVERS
(Interfacing No.2: Cut two)

2
JACKET FRONT
(Main Fabric: Cut two)
(Interlining No.1: Cut two)
(Interlining No.2: Cut two)

Centre Front

Buttonhole
positions

Hemline

11
JACKET FRONT LINING
(Lining: Cut two)

6
JACKET
FRONT FACING
(Main Fabric: Cut two)
(Interlining No.1: Cut two)

Centre Front

Buttonhole
positions

9
JACKET BACK
INTERFACING
(Interfacing No.1: Cut two)

Centre Back

(Main Fabric: Cut one on fold)
(Interlining No.1: Cut one on fold)
(Interfacing No.2: Cut one on fold)

5
TOP COLLAR

Centre Back
Place to fold
of fabric

Neck Edge
10 12 14

(Main Fabric: Cut one on fold)
(Interlining No.1: Cut one on fold)

4
UNDER COLLAR

Centre Back
Place to fold
of fabric

Shoulder
10 12 14   Neck Edge

skirt. How do you make the fabric work for both?

I always say that I am looking for a 100% build-up to a garment and no single interlining will do this on its own. We have to build up the main fabric to give it a different weight and characteristics; each layer employed will help to achieve this. So let me explain why I chose the various fabrics for the interlining layers.
Interlining No 1 Cotton mull has been chosen because we need to make the fine fabric much thicker and firm enough to tailor. If we place a firm fabric directly below the crepe de chine it will take something away from the silk; it will change the texture and give it a very hard appearance. The softness of the pure cotton will add a slight thickness but also a richness to the silk, helping to retain its softness. It will also add density, especially important for silks with light coloured backgrounds. In addition, the seam allowances will not show through by colour or ridges, because the seam allowance is not resting against the main fabric.

We've already added quite a lot to our main fabric but we still lack body. So we must use a second interlining.
Interlining No 2 (Jacket) Poult lining is a very firm fabric with lots of body. It is actually a lining fabric but we are going to use it as an interlining, which will be the base of the main fabric. Remember, interlining layers work as one with the main fabric.
Interlining No 3 (Skirt) Bremsilk is used here because the skirt does not need to be as firm as the jacket. Creases caused by sitting will fall out more easily with this softer lining.
Interfacing No 1 Duck linen – this pure linen is of medium weight and very firm. There are other types of medium weight tailoring canvas but usually made of wool, hair and other mixes. They would be far too warm for this garment.

Used as our main interfacing, this will form the 'T-zone' in the upper garment; acting as a support for the centre fronts, neck edge and revers, shoulders and armholes, extending approximately 7.5cm (3in) below the armholes (*fig.1*). Cut with a slow curve across the

shoulder blades, the interfacing also provides support in the back of the garment (*fig.2*).

Steam all linen first with lots of steam and a very high heat setting before cutting out to encourage and overcome any shrinkage.
Interfacing No 2 Holland linen – much lighter in weight than duck linen. This will only be used on the top collar and revers area of the front facing, giving a slightly richer, padded look from the front and will eliminate show-through of the seam allowance from behind.
Lining Habutai silk is the lightest lining available, perfect for a summer suit

——————— TIP ———————

I usually recommend washing crepe de chine (although the label may say dry clean only) before cutting to overcome any shrinkage. Do consider your own fabric first. The floral fabric I chose has very bright coloured flowers on a white background. Therefore I had to dry clean in this case to avoid the colours running.

————————————————

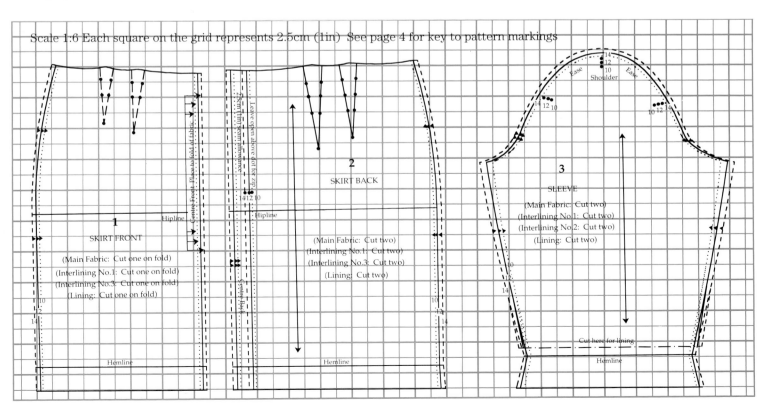

Scale 1:6 Each square on the grid represents 2.5cm (1in) See page 4 for key to pattern markings

1
SKIRT FRONT
(Main Fabric: Cut one on fold)
(Interlining No.1: Cut one on fold)
(Interlining No.3: Cut one on fold)
(Lining: Cut one on fold)

2
SKIRT BACK
(Main Fabric: Cut two)
(Interlining No.1: Cut two)
(Interlining No.3: Cut two)
(Lining: Cut two)

3
SLEEVE
(Main Fabric: Cut two)
(Interlining No.1: Cut two)
(Interlining No.2: Cut two)
(Lining: Cut two)

RIGHT: My theory on the use of interlinings is perfectly demonstrated on this tailored silk suit. You no longer need to reject a soft silk just because it doesn't have the body for your chosen pattern.

without adding any unnecessary bulk. As it is a pure, natural fibre, it will also breathe well.

Despite the numerous additional layers, you will see that we have in fact only built up the crepe de chine to a medium-weight fabric.

METHOD
JACKET
1. Cut the following pieces:
Main fabric: 1, 2, 3, 4, 5, 6, 7
Interlining No 1: 1, 2, 3, 4, 5, 6, 7
Interlining No 2: 1, 2 and 3
Interfacing No 1: 4, 8, and 9
Interfacing No 2: 5, 10
Lining: 3, 11 and 12

―――――――――― TIP ――――――――――

A useful tip when cutting out slippery silks such as crepe de chine, chiffon and satin-back crepe; fold the silk selvedge to selvedge and pin down the silk to a single layer of cotton. The static silk will cling to the hairy finish of the cotton, preventing it from sliding. Your cutting will also be clear and sharp as you cut through cotton and silk.

If you are using cotton as an interlining, do the two jobs in one, using the interlining as your cutting cloth! Ensure you have two layers of cotton and cut all four layers together.

―――――――――――――――――――――

2. Take all the silk pieces and corresponding cotton pieces. Place the cotton to the wrong side of the silk. Press them together. See how they cling due to the static. Using a Straw needle and Kinkame thread, tack all around the seam allowance, 13mm (½in) from the raw edge so as not to interfere with the machine stitching line later. Smooth all layers as you work your way round, making sure they are absolutely flat to each other.
3. *Jacket Buttonholes* Take the left side jacket front to make the bound buttonholes. Follow the Couture Technique (page 111), with one amendment (below) due to the cotton mull interlining.

On the wrong side of the garment

(cotton mull side) mark the completed buttonholes with a pencil. Now completely cut away the cotton mull from each buttonhole. *DO NOT* cut through to the main fabric. Now you can continue with the bound buttonhole instructions, placing the marked Bondaweb over the wrong side of the main fabric.

This step is necessary so that when the buttonhole edges are turned back to the wrong side, they will stick to the interlining.
4. You will now need all corresponding poult interlining sections. Match up each section for Fronts, Back and Sleeves. Tack again 13mm (½in) from the raw edge, joining interlining to the main fabric.
5. Working on the left Front, which has the buttonholes, you will need to clear the poult from the buttonhole area.

Cut a square in the poult, a fraction bigger than the piping cord area, but no larger than the fabric covering the cord. Oversew the poult in place, securing down to the covering underneath.

You should now have:
Three layers: Fronts, Back, Sleeves
Two layers: Under collar, Top collar, Front and Back Neck facing

6. Take the jacket Fronts and Back and machine in the darts. Clip into the darts, stopping just before the stitching line and press all four towards the centre.
7. *Interfacing No 1* For this design I have included separate pattern pieces for the interfacing. If using another pattern you will need to cut it from the main fabric pattern. As a guide, always remember that you need to interface the centre fronts, the revers, the neck edge, shoulder seam, armhole and 5–7.5cm (2–3in) below the arm. Shape from this point under the arm in a slow curve through the middle of the pattern, using a middle dart or seam as a marker, finishing at the hemline (*fig.1*).
8. The same applies to the back. Interface the neck edge, shoulder, armhole and 5–7.5cm (2–3in) under the

―――――――――― TIP ――――――――――

When interfacing, both front and back inside edges need to curve. If cut straight to the bust and off to the side seam, or straight across the back, the lines would show through to the main fabric. Being curved they will move around with the body.

―――――――――――――――――――――

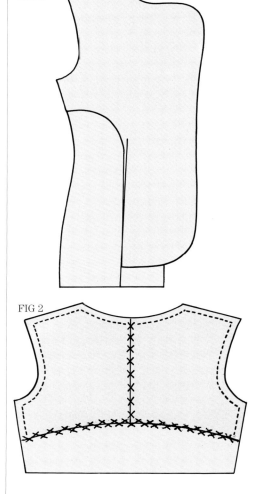

FIG 1

FIG 2

arm, curving up over the shoulder blades to the Centre Back (*fig.2*).
9. Lay each interfacing piece to the wrong side of each Front section. Tack all around the outer edge. Using a Betweens needle and Gütermann silk thread, herringbone stitch the inner edge to the poult layer only. These stitches will remain in the garment. The interfacing is now secure and will not move around.

*LEFT: This is a versatile jacket pattern: wear it with a
softly pleated skirt to create an impressive business suit.*

10. You will have to clear the duck linen from the buttonhole. Cut a square opening slightly bigger than the poult opening; hand stitch down to the poult to secure.

11. Always cut the Back interfacing with a Centre Back seam. This will allow ease when the shoulders are expanded.

Take the Back interfacing pieces and place at Top Back. Trim away about 6mm (¼in) from each side of the Centre Back seam allowance, overlap the remaining seam. Tack around the outer edge using a Betweens needle and Gütermann silk thread. Cross stitch the Centre Backs together.

12. Now herringbone stitch the inner edge to the poult layer, using Gütermann silk thread (*fig.2*).

13. Join the Fronts to the Back by machining together at shoulder seams and side seams. Machine side seams of the sleeves. Trim away the duck linen from the side and shoulder seams to 3mm (⅛in) from the stitching line. Clip side seams of jacket and sleeves. Press open all seams using the 3-Point Press.

14. *The Collar* Take the Under collar and interface with the duck linen. Interface the Top collar with the holland linen.

15. Cover a length of piping cord (Couture Techniques) long enough to go around the outer edge of the collar.

16. Lay the covered cord over the seam

TIP

Reinforce corners and points as follows. Machine an extra row of stitches across the corners immediately outside the original stitching line. Reverse at the corner by about three stitches and then machine forward again. This will reinforce the corner and will enable you to trim right up to the machine stitching so that you eliminate the bulk completely when trimming (*fig.3*).

FIG 3

allowance of the Top collar. Clipping at the corners, machine in place 3mm (⅛in) away from the cord using a piping foot on your machine.

17. With right sides together, place Under collar to Top collar. Machine outer edges together, 1.5mm (¹/₁₆in) away from the cord. Area between notches to be left open.

18. Layer the seams, cutting away bulk from the corners. Clip and turn to right side. Press. With Under collar facing right side of jacket, tack in place between •s of neck edge.

19. Now cut and cover a length of cord to run the length around the revers, and front edge; ending where the facing finishes. I recommend you cut a longer piece than required and trim later.

20. Place the covered cord so that it rests over the seam allowance of the revers and front edge of the main garment. Leave a good 13mm (½in) of extra covered cord at each end. This is tucked into the seam allowance. Clip into corners (*fig.4*) and machine in place 3mm (⅛in) from the cord.

21. *Facings* Using pattern piece 10, interface the Front facings with holland linen in the revers area only. Tack

FIG 4

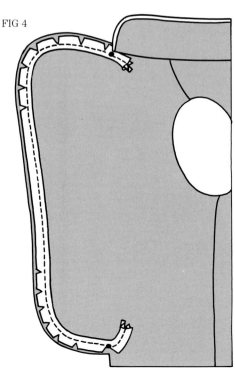

around the outer edge and herringbone stitch inner edge to the cotton mull.

22. Join Front facings to Back facing by machine stitching. Press seam open. Lay facing to jacket with right sides together, matching shoulder seams, front notches and • at hemline. Pin and machine in place, 1.5mm (¹/₁₆in) from the piping cord.

23. Following the corner tip above, layer the seam, eliminating bulk from corners and collar seam allowance at the neck edge. Clip all around. Turn to right side and press.

24. *Sleeves.* Set-in the sleeves, following the Couture Technique.

25. Add Sleeve Heads as instructed on page 119.

26. Make shoulder pads as instructed on page 119 and stitch in place.

27. *Hemming* For bottom jacket edge and sleeve hems:
Cut a strip of bias satin the length of the hem. Machine topstitch to the raw edge of all three layers of fabric.

28. Turn up the required hem, tucking the piping ends into the Front jacket facing (*fig.5*). Slipstitch the other edge of the tape to the poult layer. Repeat for the sleeves. Press lightly.

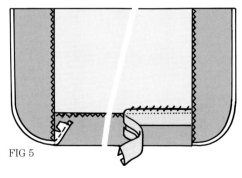

FIG 5

29. *Lining* Cut out all the lining pattern pieces in Habutai silk.

30. Join the side seams, shoulder seams and sleeve seams by machine stitching. Machine the darts. Press the darts towards the centre. Clip all seams and press open.

31. Now set in sleeves.

32. Set in the lining following the Couture Technique for Jacket Linings (page 115).

33. Lightly press the finished jacket,

LEFT AND RIGHT: The squared shoulder is a technique well worth learning as it gives a couture look to any fitted sleeve.

ensuring that the facing is lying perfectly flat to the front.

FINISHING TOUCHES

34. Complete the buttonholes as detailed on page 111. Hand stitch the buttons on the jacket front to finish.

SKIRT

1. Cut 1 and 2 from all four fabrics.
2. Take the main fabric and first interlining pieces. Press together. Add the second interlining and press.
3. Place a few pins around the seams. Tack 13mm (¹⁄₂in) from the edge, ensuring all layers are flat to each other. Now treat the three layers as one.
4. Stitch the darts in back and front. Press towards centre.
5. Machine the Centre Back seam allowance from the zip notch downwards. Iron using the 3-Point Press. Insert the zip using the technique detailed on page 121.
6. Machine the side seams. Press open.
7. Take all the lining pieces and machine to the same stage. Press all seams open. Place the lining inside the skirt, having wrong sides together.
8. Turn in the Centre Back seam around the zip, pin and slipstitch in place.
9. Machine the lining to the skirt around the waistline, 6mm (¹⁄₄in) from the edge.
10. Make two hanging loops, 51cm

(20in) long, using silk lining scraps (Couture Techniques page 116). Fold in half and machine to the side seams at waist level, with loops hanging freely downwards.
11. On this particular suit the waist will not be seen as the jacket top is intended to be worn fastened at all times. Instead of a waistband, curved petersham will sit inside the waist.

Cut a length of petersham/waistband ribbon to the required waist size plus 7.5cm (3in) for turnings. Place on top of the 15mm (⁵⁄₈in) seam allowance at the upper edge of the waist. The narrow edge of the petersham should be lying on the seam line.
12. With the right side of the skirt uppermost, turn to the Centre Back where the petersham will extend 13mm (¹⁄₂in) beyond the left edge and 6.3cm (2¹⁄₂in) beyond the right edge.

FIG 6

13. Edgestitch in place along the narrow edge of petersham (*fig.6*). Turn to the wrong side of the petersham and clip into the seam allowance up to the stitching, all the way round the waist.
14. Turn in the extending petersham at the Centre Back and hand stitch in place. Note: only turn the right extension in by 3.8cm (1¹⁄₂in), leaving a 2.5cm (1in) underlap. Turn the petersham inside the skirt, facing downwards.
15. Bar tack the edge of the petersham down to the seam at side seams, darts and either side of the zip, taking the stitches through all layers, except the main fabric.
16. Lay the hanging loops in an upright position and hand stitch in place, halfway up the petersham.
17. Close the zip and stitch two hooks and eyes to the petersham. Place the two hooks on the edge of the 2.5cm (1in) extended underlap. The eyes will lie 2.5cm (1in) along the other side for an edge-to-edge finish at Centre Back.
18. *Hem* Machine the bias satin tape to the edge of the hem through all three layers (not the skirt lining). Turn up the required hem amount and press lightly.
19. Slipstitch the edge of the tape to the second interlining layer. Bring the skirt lining down and trim to the same length as the finished skirt.
20. Turn up and press the lining 6mm (¹⁄₄in) to the wrong side. Pin the lining up to the underside of the satin tape so that the tape is invisible. Matching side seams, Centre Front and Back, slipstitch in place. Fold the lining down and press lightly.

—————————— TIP ——————————

A secured lining, that is, a lining stitched to the top of a hem, will eliminate the need to finish off seam allowances. This in turn avoids bulk and ridges. The secured lining is also unable to 'ride up' during wear.

Cutting the lining down to size only when the main skirt is complete ensures that the lining cannot possibly be too long or too short.

I've recently been scouring every available interior design shop for ideas and objects to furnish our new home. In my search I came to realize that there's an abundance of inspiration which can be transferred to dressmaking; billowing drapes, sculptured pelmets, braids and edgings. There is also a definite fashion trend to interior design and, at the time of writing, sun-dials seemed to be everywhere; golden, smiling, sun-dials which I felt could be stunning on an evening gown.

A teaching colleague and friend, Hazel, solved the problem of how to transfer the sun-dial to a gown without losing the richness of texture and colour. Her craftsmanship in Metal Thread Embroidery was the perfect medium. The rich lustre of gold metal thread combined with a raised padded foundation would give a luxurious, three-dimensional finish, that could never be overlooked.

We both agreed that the contrast between the gold embroidery and a sumptuous midnight-blue taffeta would be a striking combination. The simple cut of the gown was intentional, but I just had to add an extra touch at the top of the bodice; a subtle silhouette of clouds to complete the theme! At first glance the neckline appears to be off-the-shoulder, but in fact the back has a fairly low, strapless bodice line.

MATERIALS REQUIRED

Main fabric size 10: 5.50m (6yds) taffeta 140cm (52–54in) wide; size 12: 5.60m (6⅛yds); size 14: 5.70m (6¼yds).
Interlining No 1 size 10: 80cm (⅞yd) cotton lawn 90cm (36in) wide; size 12: 90cm (1yd); size 14: 90cm (1yd).
Interlining No 2 size 10: 80cm (⅞yd) muslin 90cm (36in) wide; size 12: 90cm (1yd); size 14: 90cm (1yd).
Firm collar and cuff canvas size 10: 80cm (⅞yd) 93cm (37in) wide; size 12: 90cm (1yd); size 14: 90cm (1yd).
Lining size 10: 6m (6½yds) Poult lining 90cm (36in) wide; size 12: 6.30m (6⅞yds); size 14: 6.50m (7⅛yds).
Petticoat size 10: 13.70m (15yds) dress net 140cm (54in) wide; size 12: 13.70m (15yds); size 14: 13.70m (15yds).

NOTIONS

4.20m (4½yds) horsehair braid
46cm (18in) zip
3.40m (3¾yds) boning

1.20m (1⅓yds) satin bias binding 2cm (¾in) wide
Petersham/waistband ribbon
The sun-dial requirements and techniques are covered separately, at the end of the gown construction.

PATTERN PIECES

Bodice: 1 Front, 2 Side Front, 3 Centre Back, 4 Side Back.
Skirt: 5 Centre Front, 6 Side Panel, 7 Centre Back, 8 Front Hem Facing, 9 Side Hem Facing, 10 Back Hem Facing.
Lining: 11 Centre Front, 12 Side Panel, 13 Centre Back, 14 Front Hem Facing, 15 Side Hem Facing, 16 Back Hem Facing.

METHODS AND TECHNIQUES

BONED BODICE
ZIP PLACEMENT
FRENCH SEAMS
INTERLINED SKIRT AND NETS
FALSE HEM
APPLICATION OF HORSEHAIR BRAID
BUILT-IN WAISTBAND
ROULEAUX LOOPS
COVERED HOOK AND BARS

My original design included gold charms around the waist and appliquéd stars on the skirt, but in the end I loved the rich simplicity of the midnight-blue taffeta.

Cut all bodice pattern pieces in main fabric, interlining 1 and 2, lining and canvas.* (*Cut without any seam allowances) Cut all skirt pieces in main fabric and dress net. Cut three net layers – one will be used as interlining. The other two will act as petticoat. Trim 5cm (2in) from the length of these.

Scale 1:6 Each square on the grid represents 2.5cm (1in)   See page 4 for key to pattern markings

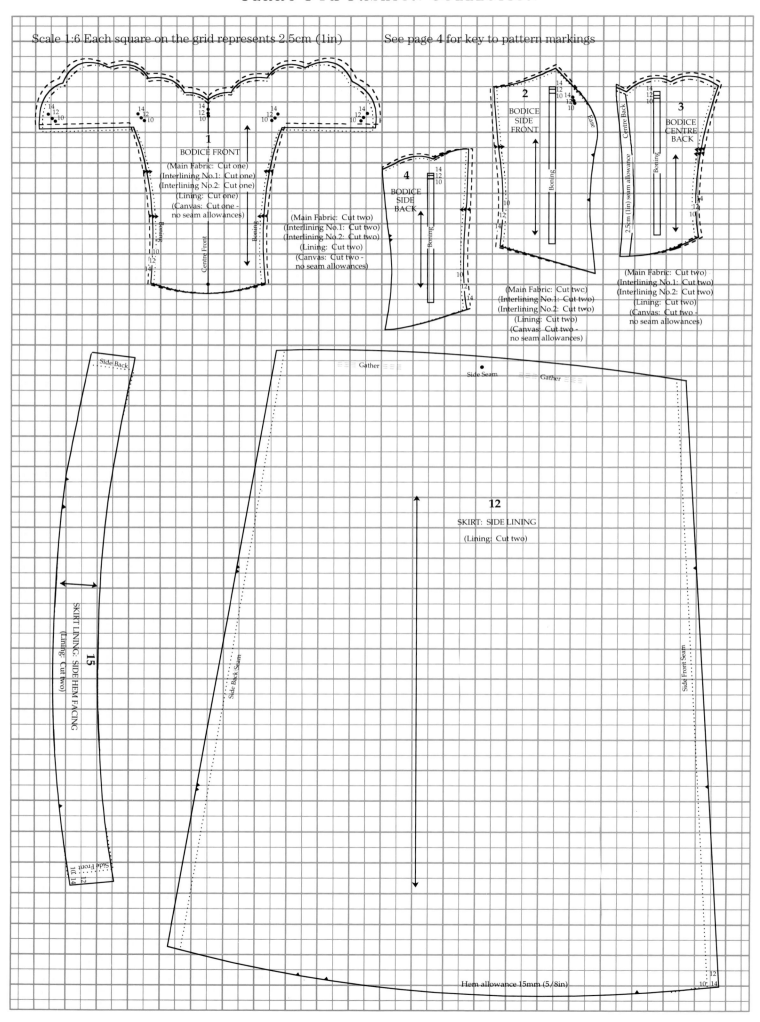

1

BODICE FRONT

(Main Fabric: Cut one)
(Interlining No.1: Cut one)
(Interlining No.2: Cut one)
(Lining: Cut one)
(Canvas: Cut one -
no seam allowances)

(Main Fabric: Cut two)
(Interlining No.1: Cut two)
(Interlining No.2: Cut two)
(Lining: Cut two)
(Canvas: Cut two -
no seam allowances)

2

BODICE
SIDE
FRONT

3

BODICE
CENTRE
BACK

4

BODICE
SIDE
BACK

(Main Fabric: Cut two)
(Interlining No.1: Cut two)
(Interlining No.2: Cut two)
(Lining: Cut two)
(Canvas: Cut two -
no seam allowances)

(Main Fabric: Cut two)
(Interlining No.1: Cut two)
(Interlining No.2: Cut two)
(Lining: Cut two)
(Canvas: Cut two -
no seam allowances)

12

SKIRT: SIDE LINING

(Lining: Cut two)

15

SKIRT LINING: SIDE HEM FACING

(Lining: Cut two)

Gather

Side Seam

Gather

Side Back Seam

Side Front Seam

Hem allowance 15mm (5/8in)

Scale 1:6 Each square on the grid represents 2.5cm (1in)
See page 4 for key to pattern markings

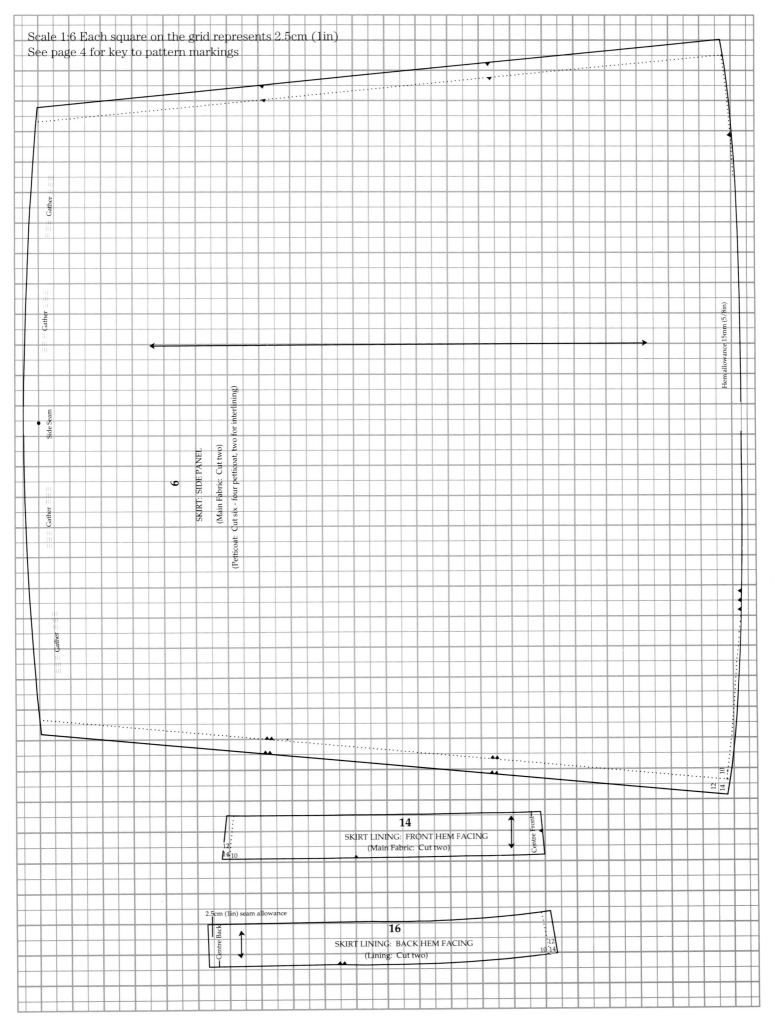

Gather

Gather

Side Seam

Gather

Gather

6

SKIRT: SIDE PANEL

(Main Fabric: Cut two)

(Petticoat: Cut six – four petticoat, two for interlining)

Hem allowance 15mm (5/8in)

12 14 10

14

SKIRT LINING: FRONT HEM FACING
(Main Fabric: Cut two)

Centre Front

12
14 10

2.5cm (1in) seam allowance

Centre Back

16

SKIRT LINING: BACK HEM FACING
(Lining: Cut two)

12
10 14

Scale 1:6 Each square on the grid represents 2.5cm (1in)   See page 4 for key to pattern markings

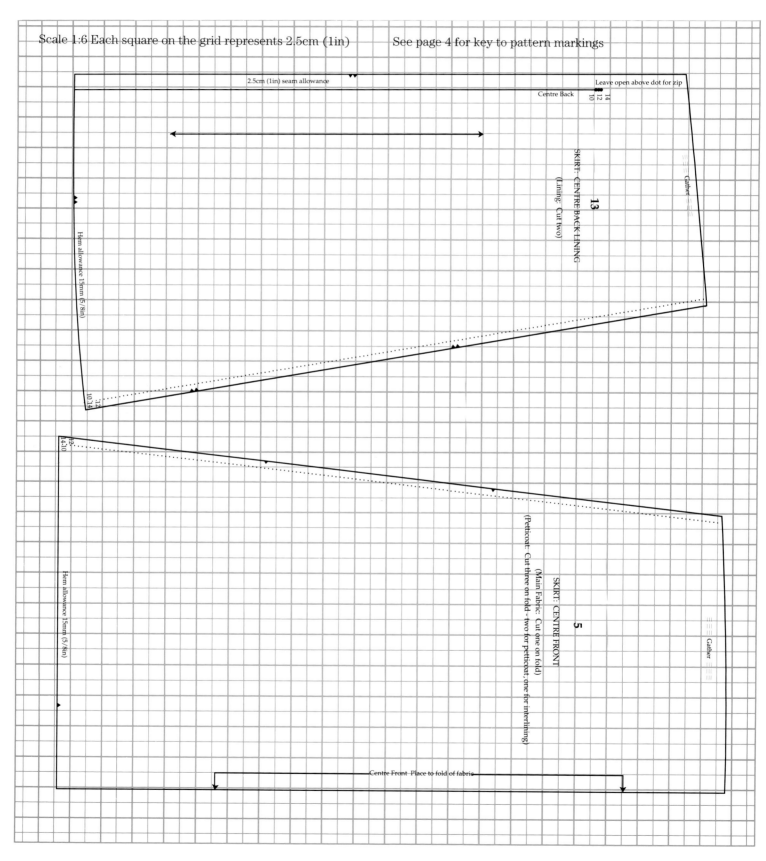

2.5cm (1in) seam allowance

Leave open above dot for zip

Centre Back

14
12
10

SKIRT: CENTRE BACK LINING

(Lining: Cut two)

13

Gather

Hem allowance 15mm (5/8in)

10 14
12

12
14 10

SKIRT: CENTRE FRONT

(Main Fabric: Cut one on fold)

(Petticoat: Cut three on fold - two for petticoat, one for interlining)

5

Gather

Hem allowance 15mm (5/8in)

Centre Front Place to fold of fabric

Scale 1:6 Each square on the grid represents 2.5cm (1in)   See page 4 for key to pattern markings

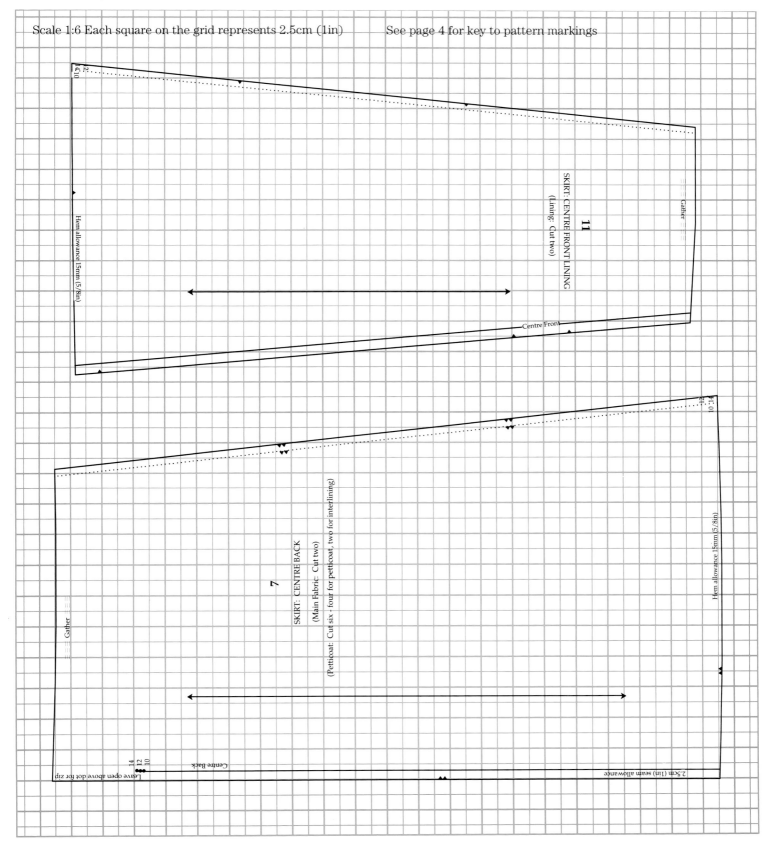

14:
4:10

Gather

11

SKIRT: CENTRE FRONT LINING

(Lining: Cut two)

Hem allowance 15mm (5/8in)

Centre Front

14:
4:10

Hem allowance 15mm (5/8in)

7

SKIRT: CENTRE BACK

(Main Fabric: Cut two)

(Petticoat: Cut six - four for petticoat, two for interlining)

Gather

14
12
10

Centre Back

Leave open above dot for zip

2.5cm (1in) seam allowance

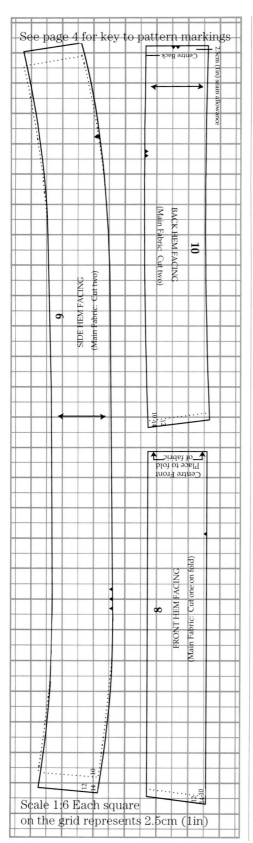

2.5cm (1in) seam allowance

Centre Back

BACK HEM FACING
(Main Fabric: Cut two)

10

SIDE HEM FACING
(Main Fabric: Cut two)

9

Place to fold
of fabric

Centre Front

FRONT HEM FACING
(Main Fabric: Cut one on fold)

8

Scale 1:6 Each square
on the grid represents 2.5cm (1in)

ABOVE AND RIGHT: *This dress has the simple foundations needed for any ballgown or wedding dress.*

If you would like more fullness in the skirt, add an extra piece of gathered net; almost like a frill. See tip on page 49 for details.

THE FABRICS

Main fabric I have used pure silk shot court taffeta. It is of medium weight in midnight-blue, shot with black. This means that the warp and weft threads are different colours. When cutting out ensure the fabric is kept in one direction at all times. The frothy body and characteristic rustle of taffeta make this an ideal fabric choice for this dramatic design.

Interlinings Interlining No 1: cotton lawn; No 2: muslin; firm collar and cuff canvas.

All the above three layers are essential for the boned bodice. Refer to the Couture Technique (page 108) for the Boned Bodice construction but note that a domette layer is not required for this particular gown.

Lining Poult lining – a firm, ribbed woven taffeta which immediately gives the wearer a sense of occasion.

Dress net A medium net used for interlining the skirt, with two added layers to form the petticoat. It serves several purposes:
• It helps to prevent the taffeta from creasing.
• Will keep the gathers full around the waistline.
• No stitches will be seen at hem level; the hem will be stitched to the net rather than the silk.
• Adds frothiness and fullness to the taffeta skirt.

METHOD
CONSTRUCTION OF BODICE

1. Follow the Basic Boned Bodice technique, noting the points below as you work through the instructions.

When placing the first piece of boning to each panel (end of Stage One), you will be aware of the extension to the Centre Front panel at neck level. This will also need boning support. Place as follows:

2. Cut a length of boning to run through the length of the extension, but staying within the canvas boundaries (*fig.1*). Machine all four sides of the boning.

FIG 1

3. Now cut a length of boning to join the Centre Front and extension boning. Overlap this at both ends; if you only just meet the other boning you will cause a weak point. Machine all four sides (*fig.1*).

4. Follow the Couture Technique through to Stage Six, noting that at Stage Four you will only join the Side Fronts to Centre Front up to the large
• . The satin tape casing and boning will also stop at this point (*fig.2*).

5. Complete the sun-dial embroidery (pages 50 to 55) before positioning it on the bodice. Once complete, position, secure and outline as instructed to blend the outer edges into the bodice.

FIG 2

LEFT: Sun-dials are very popular motifs. Try reducing the pattern and applying it to a pocket or even to a cushion front.

6. Machine the side seams of the bodice together.

7. Join all the bodice lining pieces together. Clip and press.

8. With right sides together, place the lining to the bodice, matching raw edges. Pin in place along the front neckline between the small •s. Machine 3mm (¹/₈in) outside the canvas edge, following the curve of the clouds and pivoting at all points (*fig.3*). Reinforce all points by machining an extra row into each point and out again (*fig.4*). Clip close to the stitching line.

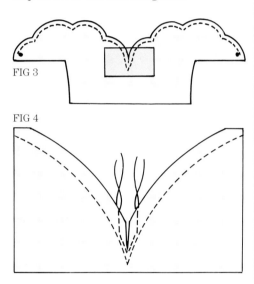

FIG 3

FIG 4

9. Now pin the rest of the bodice lining to the upper bodice edge. Start at the Centre Back matching all seam lines, finishing at the small • at the bustline on the front side panel (*fig.5*). Machine 3mm (¹/₈in) outside the canvas edge, noting from *fig.5* where stitching should end. Clip the seam up to the stitching line.

FIG 5

10. Turn the lining through to the right side. Turn in the remaining unstitched seam allowances on lower extension edge and bustline, slipstitch together. The bodice should now be complete and ready for the skirt.

SKIRT

1. Mount the corresponding pieces of main fabric to the net interlining layer. Secure together around all edges using Kinkame thread and a Straw needle.

2. Machine stitch all skirt panels together using the method for French Seams (Couture Techniques page 114). On the Centre Back seamline remember there is a 2.5cm (1in) seam allowance and leave the zip opening free. Press all seams lightly.

3. Create a false hem using pattern pieces 8, 9 and 10, following the directions in Couture Techniques.

4. Take the second layer of dress net and join all seams together by overlapping the net at seamlines and machining flat. Leave a 25cm (10in) opening at the Centre Back. Repeat for the third layer of dress net.

5. Join all skirt lining panels together, again using a French seam finish. Press. Leave an opening for the zip at the Centre Back seam.

6. Add a false hem to the skirt lining (use pattern pieces 14, 15 and 16) with

---

TIP

Using a long, loose machine stitch make three rows of stitching, the first approximately 1.5mm (¹/₁₆in) to the left of the seam line, the second 3mm (¹/₈in) to the right of the seam line and another 3mm (¹/₈in) above that. If working with fine fabric such as chiffon, keep all gathering lines to the right of the seam line so that the needle marks will not show on the outside of the garment. Pull up all three rows of stitching together for even gathers. If the gathered seam allowance is getting bulky, machine a second line 6mm (¹/₄in) from the first seam line and trim up to this second line. Neaten the edge with a machine zigzag.

TIP

To add extra fullness to the skirt, measure from the hemline to a point two-thirds of the way up. This will be the required width of the net. Now measure around the skirt and multiply by three. This will give you the length of net required.

Machine join the two ends of net and gather around the upper edge. Pin it to the net petticoat so that the bottom edge of the frill is level with the hemline and machine in place, along the upper edge. For best results, attach the frill to the uppermost layer of net petticoat.

---

the addition of horsehair braid for stiffness (Couture Techniques).

7. Gather the waistline of the main fabric skirt following the tip (left) for evenly-spaced gathers.

8. Open the Centre Back seam of the skirt and bodice flat. With right sides together, place the skirt to the bodice all around the waistline, matching Centre Fronts and seamlines. Pull up the skirt gathering threads to fit and pin in line with the gathers.

9. Turn over so bodice (wrong side) is uppermost. Machine the two together, 3mm (¹/₈in) outside of the canvas edge. Remove the pins from underneath as you work.

10. Check the bodice Centre Back to ensure it is of equal length and that both sides of the zip opening are of the same length. Adjust if necessary.

11. Complete the zip insertion following the Couture Technique.

12. *Net Petticoat* (See also tip above) Gather the upper edge of one layer of dress net. Place the seam allowance to the wrong side of the main skirt upper edge, matching notches and seamlines. Machine in place.

Repeat to attach the last layer of dress net.

13. Gather the waistline of the skirt lining. Matching Centre Front notches and Centre Backs, place right side of lining towards wrong side of the main skirt. Clipping at the bottom of the zip opening if necessary, turn in the 2.5cm

RIGHT: The sun-dial embroidery in detail.

BELOW: This neckline can be re-cut to any shape. I've imagined clouds but you could try a floral shape or perhaps angel's wings.

(1in) seam allowance around the zip, pin and slipstitch in place.

14. Machine the lining to the main skirt seam at waist. Machine a second row in the seam through all thicknesses. Trim next to the stitching line. Now, with a medium open zigzag stitch, machine over the edge all the way round to flatten the bulk.

15. Using a double thread and Straw needle, firmly overstitch the waist seam allowance down through all thicknesses to the muslin layer of the bodice. Use the canvas edge to define the waistline.

16. Bring down the bodice lining to meet the skirt lining, turning in raw edges at the zip opening and waistline. Pin in place then prickstitch to secure.

FINISHING TOUCHES

17. Finish the Centre Back with a large covered hook and bar at the top of the zip (Couture Techniques) and a smaller hook and bar tack just under the zip at waist level.

18. This rather weighty gown now requires a built-in waistband to help it sit comfortably and prevent the bodice being pulled downwards. Use the method described on page 121.

19. Make hanging loops from scraps of the lining fabric and secure them to the inside of the bodice (Couture Techniques page 116). For rouleau loop placement and length, follow the same instructions found in the Beautiful Pink Ballgown (page 98).

METAL THREAD EMBROIDERY

The embroidery design on the bodice of this gown has been worked by Hazel Everett. Here she details the equipment, types of thread and stitches that have been used. The majority of the design was worked as a separate piece and then stitched onto the bodice after interlining and boning, but before it was lined.

Metal Thread embroidery involves the laying down of metal threads within a design area and securing them with tiny, almost invisible, couching stitches. Some metal threads are hollow and are attached in the same way you would attach beading to a garment.

This type of embroidery is not recommended for beginners in needlework.

The sun-dial design has been padded with felt to give a raised effect. The face of the sun-dial is made up of a gold satin fabric with quilted facial features. The arrows were stitched directly on the bodice, as was the numerical symbol. A row of couched blue stranded cotton surrounds the edge of the sun-dial to conceal the join and to sharpen up the outline with a shadow effect.

EQUIPMENT

Acid-free tissue paper – used to protect the embroidery whilst it is being worked upon.

Air-tight tin to store metal threads.

Awl/Stiletto – a tool with a long, cylindrical sharp point, used to manipulate the metal threads.

Beeswax – used to strengthen and smooth out those threads used to sew down the design.

Mellore – a specialist tool having one smooth, rounded end and one with a long, sharp point (*fig. 1*). Used to position and manoeuvre the metal threads.

Metal Beads to finish the design, placed around the face. Hazel used four types: two, very small, round metal beads, gold-coloured glass beads (approximately 25gms of each), and

small, diamond-shaped metal beads (12 of these).

Metal Threads: (American thread equivalents with approximate sizes are given in brackets)

- 25gms (approx. 15m/16½yds) Pearl Purl size 2 (Jaceron size 8)
- Bright Check Purl (Frieze Brilliant) 10gms (approx 7m/7¾yds) size 8 (small)
10gms (approx 4.5m/5yds) size 5 (medium)
10gms (approx 10m/11yds) size 2 (large)
- 25gms (approx 15m/16½yds) Rough Purl size 6 (Bullion Matte size 7)
- 25gms (approx 15m/16½yds) Smooth Purl size 6 (Bullion Brilliant size 7)
One reel (approx 45m/49¼yds) Imitation Jap T69 (Japan Thread, middle size)

Needles – use Crewel No 9 and No 10 for attaching the metal threads and Crewel No 1 for pulling through the ends of the metal threads. (A tapestry needle may be used but you must first make a hole in the fabric with the awl.)

Scissors – an old pair for cutting the metal threads and a second pair for cutting the embroidery threads.

Square frame – to hold the fabric taut. If used with a pair of tressles it allows the use of both hands.

Thimbles – use either metal or leather.

Threads – use any domestic thread to attach the metal threads to the fabric, for couching and when stitching the design to the bodice; for example, Gütermann multi-purpose thread. Always wax before use and choose a colour similar to the metal thread for invisibility.

Gold Anchor Stranded Cotton for facial features of sun-dial.

Tweezers – a flat-ended pair for turning and squeezing the metal threads is essential.

Velvet/Patty Board – the velvet will cushion the metal threads whilst they are being cut.

PADDING MATERIALS AND FABRICS

Felt – used to pad the main sun-dial motif. Different heights can be achieved

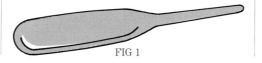
FIG 1

An appliquéd design in silks could look equally effective on this bodice.

by attaching additional layers. The centre of the sun-dial has eight layers of felt, whilst the edges go down to one. It is important that the largest layer is attached last, to create a smooth effect for the gold to rest on.

Bump – Soft cotton embroidery thread (e.g. Anchor/DMC) that is used to raise small areas of metal threads. On the sun-dial design it is used to pad the straight rays. Several bundles of soft cotton are couched down to create the padded effect.

Supporting background fabric – use either pre-washed calico, sheeting or additional foreground fabric. Hazel used organza, as the whole design was padded and this supported the metal threads. The use of such a fine fabric reduces the problem of too much

bulk when the design is attached to the bodice.

Foregound fabric – plain colours create the boldest effect and reduce the possibility of clashing with the metal threads. You can use pure silk (Thai, taffeta, lightly-textured dupion, tussah and shantung), wool mixtures, cottons or velvet.

Satin fabric – for the sun-dial face.

TYPES OF METAL THREADS

Embroidery threads containing goldplated wires can be divided into two basic types; all metal materials, such as Purls (which are hollow threads) and 'spun' metallic threads, such as Couching threads, which are solid.

Wires used to make purls are a combination of gold upon silver, or gold

upon a thin layer of silver which is on top of a copper alloy. Spun metallic threads, such as couching threads, are a simple combination of flattened goldplated wire lapped upon a yarn of silk, cotton or synthetic fibre.

A wide variety is available to the needleworker but we detail only those threads used on the sun-dial. Hazel used mainly hollow metal threads on the design to reduce the amount of threads that required pulling through the fabric and neatening off at the back. This reduced stress on the garment fabric since many couching threads are very thick and make large holes.

Imitation Jap (Japan Thread) A modern equivalent of Jap made from an alloy. This was used towards the edge of the design, two threads couched down together in a brick pattern. Jap was originally available in 18ct but is now very rare. It consists of a narrow strip of beaten metal wrapped around an orange silk core.

Purls All the threads are cut to short lengths and are threaded like beads, with the exception of pearl purl. None of the purl metal thread should pass through to the back of the fabric as the threads are all cut to fit the exact shape of the design. Purls are available in a variety of sizes. In most cases, the larger the product reference number, the smaller the metal thread (applicable to UK numbering system only).

Smooth Purl/Bullion Brilliant A very shiny hollow thread, available in several sizes. Size 6 (7) was used for the embroidery in a graded satin stitch formation on the straight rays. Contrasts well with rough purl.

Rough Purl/Bullion Matte Dull or matt in appearance. Size 6 (7) was used on the sun-dial, also in a graded satin stitch formation. This thread could also be used for stem stitch or other techniques if so required.

Bright Check Purl/Frieze Brilliant A shiny spirally-textured thread, available in several sizes. This was cut into tiny pieces for check chips and cut into approximately 6mm (¼in) lengths for

the stem stitch on the numeral XII.
Pearl Purl/Jaceron Sometimes called
bead purl as it resembles a row of
beads. It is available in several sizes and
needs to be slightly stretched before
use so as to create narrow grooves in
which to place the couching stitches.

An excellent outlining thread, it is
very stiff and can be used to create
sharp edges, or pinched with tweezers
to make fine points. Size 2 (8) was used
on the sun-dial but much smaller sizes
are available for smaller designs.

ATTACHING METAL THREADS

Pearl Purl Slightly stretch the pearl
purl to form narrow grooves. Position it
so that the end meets the edge of the
design as none of the thread should
pass through to the back of the fabric.
Couch over the metal, coming up on the
outside and going down on the inside,
almost in the same spot (*fig.2*). Gently
pull on each stitch so that it disappears
between the grooves. It usually makes a
popping noise as it goes through. Place
a stitch in the first and last couple of
grooves to securely anchor the pearl
purl. All other couching stitches are
made approximately 3mm (^{1}/$_8$in) apart.
The only exception is when difficult
areas, such as sharp points are fastened
down. Then the stitches need to be
closer together. Cut the spare pearl purl
off when couching is almost complete.

FIG 2

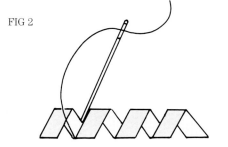

*Jap/Japan Thread and other
Couched Threads* For the threads we
have used, couching stitches are placed
straight over the metal thread.

The finer threads are frequently
couched down two at a time. Leave
ends of approximately 5cm (2in)
overhanging the design. Make couching
stitches every 3mm (^{1}/$_8$in) along the

length of the metal thread. Angle the
needle to 45 degrees when couching
over the threads. This helps to reduce
any gaps between rows as the threads
can slide up closer to each other. Using
a brick pattern also creates a smoother
appearance (*fig.3*).

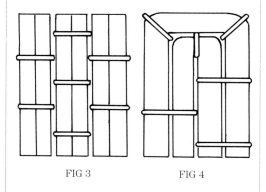

FIG 3　　　　　FIG 4

A brick pattern is where the second
row is placed in between the stitches of
the first. Turn the edges or corners
wherever possible as it is more
economical of thread and time. To turn,
make a stitch in each corner of the
outside thread to square off the edges
(*fig.4*). A single horizontal stitch is
placed over the inside thread to hold
that down. Often it is necessary to twist
the thread as it is couched down to stop
the core becoming uncovered. This is
essential when using Jap.

To take down the ends, make a hole
in the fabric with an awl and thread the
Jap into a large-eyed needle. (Use a
very large crewel/tapestry needle.)
Carefully pull the needle through to the
back of the fabric and secure the thread
underneath the embroidered area. This
helps to hide any unsightly bulk.

*Rough, Smooth and Check
Purl/Bullion Matte, Bullion Brilliant
and Frieze Brilliant* All are stitched in
the same manner. The metal threads
are carefully cut to fit the design shape
exactly. Treat these metal threads as
flexible beads and sew them down by
pushing the waxed thread through the
centre of the metal lengths. These
metal threads can be formed into
different patterns. They can either be
made into satin or stem stitch (which
was used on the numeral XII), or cut

into small pieces (chips) for close
seeding.

Satin Stitch The metal threads can be
cut into identical lengths for bands or
into graded lengths to cover shapes
(*fig.5*). They are sewn down so that the
metal threads lie parallel to each other
and they can either be sewn down flat
or over padding.

FIG 5

Stem Stitch (*fig.6*) Cut the metal
threads to identical lengths, about 6mm
(^{1}/$_4$in). Fasten on a waxed sewing
thread. Push one of the metal lengths
onto this thread. Make a straight stitch
and bring the needle up through the
fabric, half-way along the metal thread.
Place another metal length onto the
needle and make a second straight
stitch. Again, bring the needle out
through the fabric half-way along the
metal length and make sure that the
needle is always brought out on the
same side of the stitch. Continue in this
way until the design area is complete. A
half length could be placed at each end
to neaten the stitchery.

FIG 6

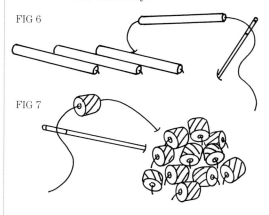

FIG 7

Seeding (*fig.7*) Cut the check purl into
tiny pieces (chips) approximately
1.5mm (^{1}/$_{16}$in) long. Sew the chips down
randomly, so that the spirals do not lie
in the same direction. Position them
very close together to produce a flat,
completely covered surface.

SUN-DIAL METHOD

1. Enlarge and transfer the main outline of the design without the arrows and numerals to the organza.

2. Pad the main design area with eight layers of felt, making sure that the last layer is the largest to eliminate any ridges on the surface.

3. Cut a circle, approximately 10cm (4in) in diameter, from the gold satin fabric. Pin the circle to the main design.

4. Work the facial features in backstitch through all layers using single strands of cotton. Secure the outer edge of the circle to the organza. Trim the raw edge which will later be concealed by the small beads.

5. Couch the pearl purl to form the outer edges of the straight rays, starting from the bottom tip.

6. Surround the inner edge of pearl purl with Imitation Jap, in a brick pattern.

7 Add a second row of pearl purl to section off the Imitation Jap.

8. Pad the straight rays with bump.

LEFT: You could use these stitch techniques to create an interesting edging for an evening jacket.

9. Work a graded satin stitch over the bump, using rough and smooth purl alternately.

10. Pearl purl the outer edges of the curved rays.

11. Couch a brick pattern over the Imitation Jap on the inner edge of the pearl purl line.

12. Repeat another row of pearl purl to border the Imitation Jap.

13. Using check chips/seeding, fill in the area from the tip of the ray up to the sun-dial face. Start with the smallest size at the tip and allocate roughly a third of the area to each chip size.

14. Sew down the assorted beads and any extra check chips at random around the quilted face.

15. Trim the organza to within 10mm (³/₈in) of the metal thread work. Attach the sun-dial to the bodice and edge with a line of midnight-blue, couched stranded cotton.

16. Work the arrows directly onto the bodice using Imitation Jap, pearl purl and check chips.

17. Work the numeral directly onto the bodice in stem stitch, using bright check purl.

KEY TO EMBROIDERY
1 satin face with features quilted in backstitch
2 variety of metal beads and check chips
3 imitation jap, T69, couched in brick pattern
4 couched pearl purl edge, size 2
5 smooth purl, size 6, in satin stitch
6 rough purl, size 6, in satin stitch
7,8,9 bright check purl, sizes 2, 5 and 8, largest size nearest to the face gradually fading out to smallest size on the tips
10 check chips
11 bright check purl, size 6, in stem stitch

Note: The above outline has been reduced by half – each square on the grid represents 1cm (³/₈in). To enlarge, see page 8.

LOUNGE SUIT AND FLOPPY APPLIQUÉD HAT

I think clothes are fun and I, for one, just love dressing up! I believe there's an outfit for every occasion, but for most of us the realities of life do not allow for such luxuries!

For those of us fortunate enough to make our own garments, we at least have the ability to create something totally original. You can choose whatever fabric design you wish to make up this lounge suit and matching hat, for example, choose patterns for casual wear or plain colours for work. Just be sure you have fun when you wear it!

MATERIALS REQUIRED (SIZES 10–14)
All three garment sizes can be cut from the same yardage due to the width of the fabrics chosen.

BLOUSE
Main fabric: 2.20m (2⅜yds) patterned silk crepe de chine 115cm (44–45in) wide
Interlining: 2m (2¼yds) plain silk crepe de chine 115cm (44–45in) wide
Interfacing: 15cm (6in) strip silk organza 115cm (44–45in) wide

─────── TIP ───────
If you are short on time, it is not strictly necessary to interline the blouse, but it will add weight and density.

TROUSERS
These are loose, fun trousers with an elasticated waist. I have not interlined them due to the softness of fabric and width of the trouser leg. The silk I have used is light in colour and ideally should have density added. However, the

problems of doing so, because of the design, outweigh the reasons for interlining.
Main fabric: 2.20m (2⅜yds) plain silk crepe de chine 115cm (44–45in) wide.

NOTIONS
5 buttons (to cover) 15mm (⅝in) diameter
Elastic 3.2cm (1¼in) wide – waist measurement plus 2.5cm (1in).

PATTERN PIECES
1 Blouse Front, 2 Blouse Back, 3 Sleeve, 4 Front Facing, 5 Back Neck Facing, 6 Cuff, 7 Sleeve Binding, 8 Trouser Front, 9 Trouser Back, 10 Trouser Pocket, 11 Trouser Waistband.

METHOD
BLOUSE
1. Cut 1, 2, 3, 4, 5, 6 and 7 in main fabric; 1, 2 and 3 in interlining; no 6 in interfacing.
2. Machine main fabric Fronts to Back at shoulder seams. Repeat for interlining pieces. Press seams open.
3. Pin sleeves in place by matching up

─────── TIP ───────
Match up the pattern for the Centre Front. This will make all the difference between a couture garment and a homemade or commercial garment.

It is not possible to cut two fronts side by side if you have a random pattern. Concentrate on the pattern at the Centre Front line, not the front edge.

Take the first pattern piece, for example, the Left Front. Cut out the piece and then mark the centre line. You must match up this centre line on the Right Front but remember to lay the pattern piece in the opposite direction, otherwise you will cut two left Fronts!

METHODS AND TECHNIQUES
CUTTING FINE FABRICS
INTERLINING
SLEEVE OPENINGS AND CUFFS
MACHINED OR HAND-WORKED
BUTTONHOLES
CURVED HEMS
ZIGZAG SEAM FINISH
ELASTICATED WAISTBAND
HONG KONG FINISH
COVERING BUTTONS
APPLIQUÉ

RIGHT: This suit is, I think, the most versatile in the book. With its matching hat, it's suitable for any age and any event.

Scale 1:6 Each square on the grid represents 2.5cm (1in)
See page 4 for key to pattern markings

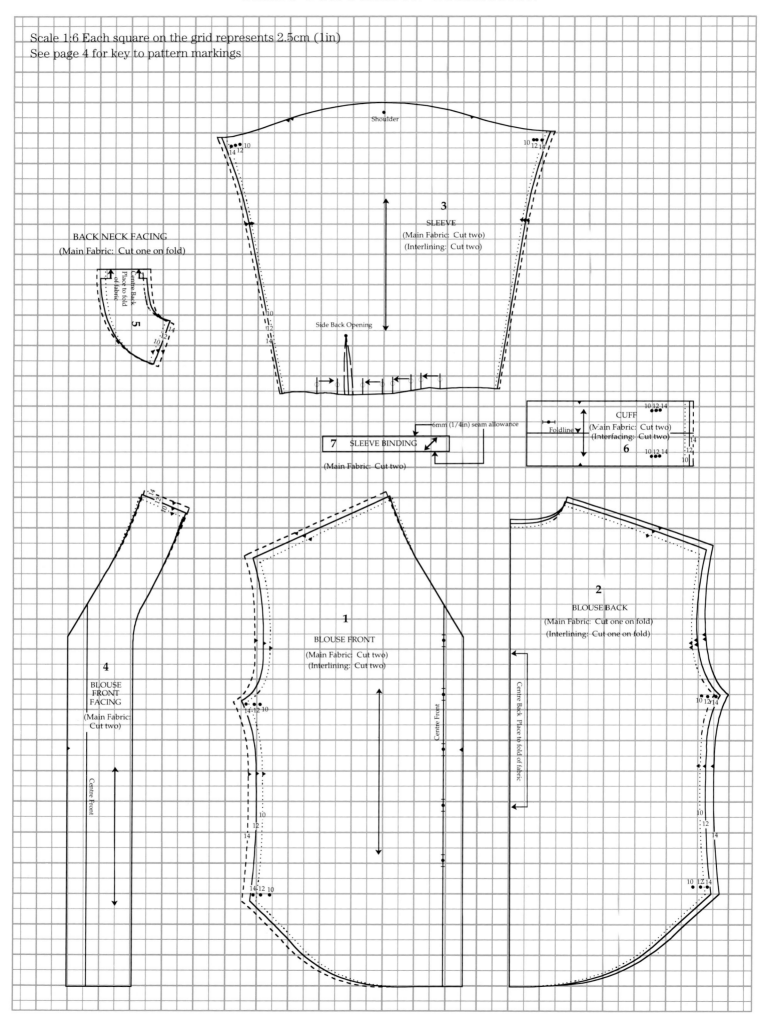

Shoulder

3
SLEEVE
(Main Fabric: Cut two)
(Interlining: Cut two)

BACK NECK FACING
(Main Fabric: Cut one on fold)

Centre Back
Place to fold of fabric

5

10
12
14

Side Back Opening

10
12
14

6mm (1/4in) seam allowance

CUFF
(Main Fabric: Cut two)
(Interfacing: Cut two)

Foldline

6

10 12 14

10 12 14

7 SLEEVE BINDING

(Main Fabric: Cut two)

10 12 14

2
BLOUSE BACK
(Main Fabric: Cut one on fold)
(Interlining: Cut one on fold)

1

BLOUSE FRONT

(Main Fabric: Cut two)
(Interlining: Cut two)

Centre Front

Centre Back Place to fold of fabric

4

BLOUSE
FRONT
FACING

(Main Fabric:
Cut two)

Centre Front

14 12 10

10
12
14

10 12 14

10 12 14

10
12
14

14 12 10

10 12 14

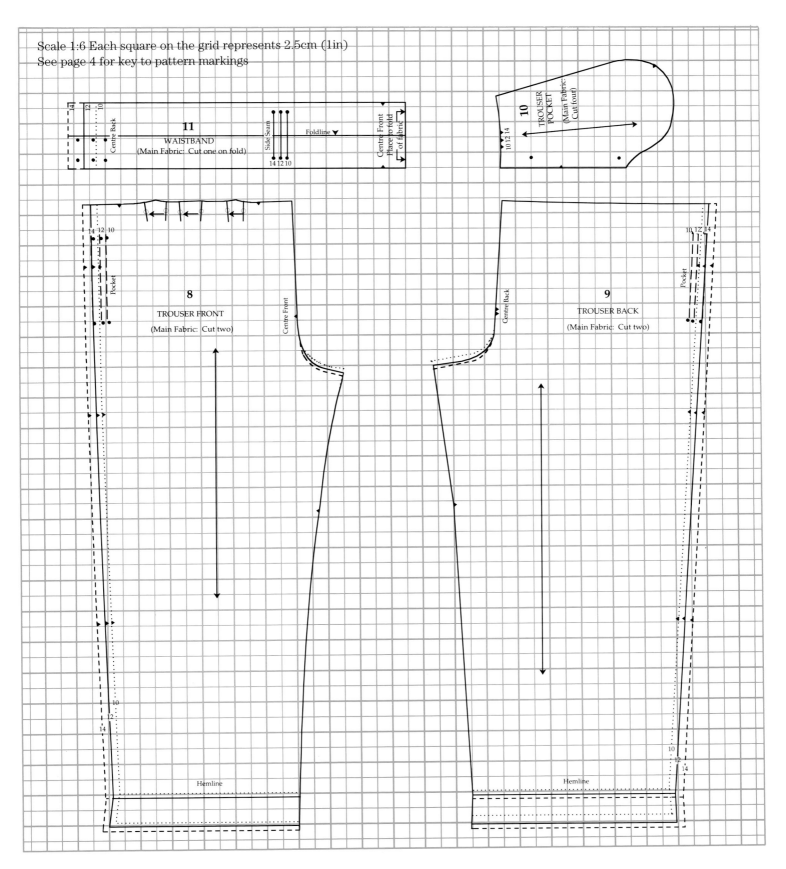

Scale 1:6 Each square on the grid represents 2.5cm (1in)
See page 4 for key to pattern markings

11
WAISTBAND
(Main Fabric: Cut one on fold)

10
TROUSER POCKET
(Main Fabric: Cut four)

8
TROUSER FRONT
(Main Fabric: Cut two)

9
TROUSER BACK
(Main Fabric: Cut two)

LEFT: Each piece, including the hat, can be made in almost any fabric. The suit is comfortable to wear but smart enough, with its matching hat, to wear on formal occasions.

shoulder seams, front and back notches. Machine, taking usual seam allowance.
4. Repeat with the interlining pieces. Press the seam towards the sleeve.
5. Machine join side seams from sleeve edge through to notch at the top of the curved hemline. Clip the underarm seam for ease.
6. Repeat with the interlining pieces. Press all seams open.
7. Place the interlining inside blouse, wrong sides facing together. Machine 6mm (¼in) inside all the raw edges, that is, sleeve hem, hemline, front edge and neckline. This will prevent movement. Now treat as one layer.
8. Using additional interlining fabric follow the Couture Technique to complete the Curved Hem. Complete both Front and Back hems, extending 2.5cm (1in) beyond the • at the side seam. Tuck in the raw edge and secure with hand stitching (*fig.1*).

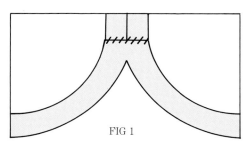

FIG 1

9. Join Front and Back facing at shoulder seam. Press seam open.
10. Place the facing on blouse Front and neck edge with right sides together, matching up shoulder seams. Pin and machine a 15mm (⅝in) seam. Layer the seam and clip around the neckline. Press the seam flat, then press back to the wrong side.
11. At the bottom edge of the facing turn under 15mm (⅝in) to meet the hemline.
12. Turn in 15mm (⅝in) along the entire outer edge of the facing, clipping where necessary. Press. Pin the facing down to the interlining only, matching hem and shoulder seam. Check that the facing is lying absolutely flat to the main fabric. Slipstitch to the interlining, all the way round the outer edge of the facing. Press lightly.

13. *Side Back Opening on Sleeve.* Machine a line from the sleeve hemline up to the •, stitching back down again to the hemline, 6mm (¼in) from the first stitching line. Cut up to the •.
   Follow the Hong Kong Finish technique (page 115), using main fabric and pattern piece 7, to bind the opening.
14. Matching the symbols transferred from the paper pattern, make the pleats at the hemline, pressing them towards the opening (*fig.2*). Pin in place, then machine 6mm (¼in) from the edge to secure.

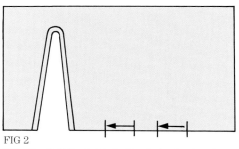

FIG 2

15. *Cuff.* Blindstitch the interfacing to the main fabric along the foldline for stability during wash and wear. Tack around the outer edge.
16. Fold right sides together along the foldline. Form the underlap of the cuff by machining the 15mm (⅝in) seam allowance at the side of the cuff, pivot at the corner and machine to the •. Clip down to the • on the underside of the cuff only. Press down the seam allowance and machine the other side. Stitch across the corners to reinforce them (*fig.3*). Layer the seam allowance and eliminate any bulk.
17. Turn the cuff through to right side and press. Position cuff on the bottom of the sleeve hemline, right sides together, matching up notches. The

FIG 3

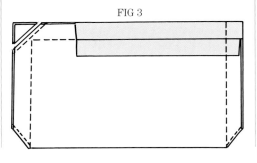

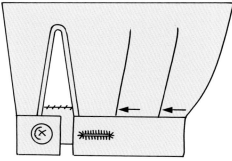

FIG 4

underlap will always lay on the 'short side' of the seam (*fig.4*). Machine. Press the 15mm (⅝in) seam towards the cuff. Bring the folded seam up to rest against the first machine line to complete the cuff. Slipstitch in place and press.
18. *Buttons and Buttonholes* Machine stitch buttonholes, using the pattern markings for position guideline. If you prefer, follow the Couture Technique for hand sewn buttonholes.

——————— TIP ———————

For the finishing touch, cover your own buttons. I used plastic buttons – they have a rounder, softer appearance for the silk fabric. Follow the manufacturer's instructions for covering and stitch to the garment.
   Try wetting the silk fabric before covering the button; it is then much easier to place it on the button mould. Consider your patterned fabric when covering buttons. Try to match the design – this will give your garment a far more professional finish.

TROUSERS
1. Cut two trouser Fronts and Backs, four pockets and one waistband in main fabric.
2. With right sides together, place one pocket to each side of the trouser leg. Machine along straight edge. Finish each seam using the zigzag technique (page 121) as an alternative to overlocking. Press towards the pocket.
3. Pin trouser Front to Back having pockets open flat to the side. Machine around the pockets, joining the two

together to form the pocket. Neaten the seam. Now machine the outside leg seam from waist level to the first •, and from lower pocket • to hemline. Machine the inside leg seam. Finish all seams with zigzag stitching and press.

Clip up to the lower • at the pocket before zigzagging. The pocket will then lay to the front and the side seam to the back.

4. Fold the pocket towards the front. Fold and press in the pleats toward the side seams and machine 6mm (¹/₄in) from raw edge to secure in place.

5. Pin the crotch seam by matching up the underleg notches. Machine, neaten raw edges and press.

6. *Waistband* Machine the Centre Back seam of the waistband, leaving open between •s. Press open the seam. The opening for the elastic will be on the inside of the waistband and the waistband seam will match the Centre Back seam on the trousers.

7. With right sides together, pin waistband to waistline, matching front and side notches. Machine the seam allowance.

8. Press under the 15mm (⁵/₈in) seam allowance on the outer edge of the waistband. Bring over the outer edge to the inside to cover the seam and to meet the row of machine stitching. Pin and slipstitch in place.

9. Cut the elastic to the required waist measurement. Allow a comfortable fit plus 2.5cm (1in) for joining. Thread the elastic through ensuring that it lies flat at all times. Overlap the two ends by 2.5cm (1in) and machine as shown (*fig.5*) for a secure and flat finish. Slipstitch the opening.

FIG 5

10. *Hem* Turn under 15mm (⁵/₈in) at hem level and press. Turn up this hem a further 3.2cm (1¹/₄in). Press again. Machine edgestitch along the top of the hem. Finally, to make a feature of this, stitch a second line 6mm (¹/₄in) inside the first.

TERRY FOX FASHION COLLECTION

FLOPPY APPLIQUÉD HAT

DESIGN NO. 6

MATERIALS REQUIRED

Material requirements will be the same for the three hat sizes given: small, medium or large.

Main fabric: 1.70m (1⁷/₈yds) plain silk crepe de chine 115cm (44–45in) wide

Interlining No 1: 80cm (⁷/₈yd) firm weight interfacing (e.g. Vilene) 90cm (36in) wide

Interlining No 2: 60cm (²/₃yd) light to medium-weight canvas 93cm (37in) wide (no seam allowances required)

NOTIONS

Suitable pieces from the patterned crepe de chine for flowers Bondaweb/Vliesofix/Wonder Under 65cm (26in) curved petersham or waistband ribbon

PATTERN PIECES

1 Brim, 2 Crown, 3 Side Band, 4 Side Drape

METHOD

Cut two pieces 1, 2 and 3 in main fabric
Cut one piece 4 in main fabric
Cut one piece 1, 2 and 3 interlining No 1
Cut one piece 1 and 2 interlining No 2 (without any seam allowances)

1. *Brim* Place the canvas on top of the Vilene. Press together. Machine 3mm

FIG 1

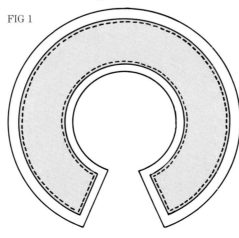

(¹/₈in) inside the canvas edge (*fig.1*) to secure.

2. Place these layers on the wrong side of the Upper silk brim, Vilene facing the silk, and machine 6mm (¹/₄in) outside the canvas edge.

3. Machine the Centre Back seams of the Upper and Lower brim. Press open.

4. Lay brims right sides together, matching up seams and notches. Machine all round the outer edge of the brim, just outside the canvas.

5. Cut the Vilene away from the seam allowance and trim the rest of the seam to 6mm (¹/₄in).

6. Turn to right side and press, ensuring that the seam is laying sharp on the outer edge. Bring the inside seams to meet and tack in place (*fig.2*).

7. Edgestitch the brim, starting at the Centre Back. Then topstitch 13mm (¹/₂in) apart, working your way to the inner brim (*fig.3*).

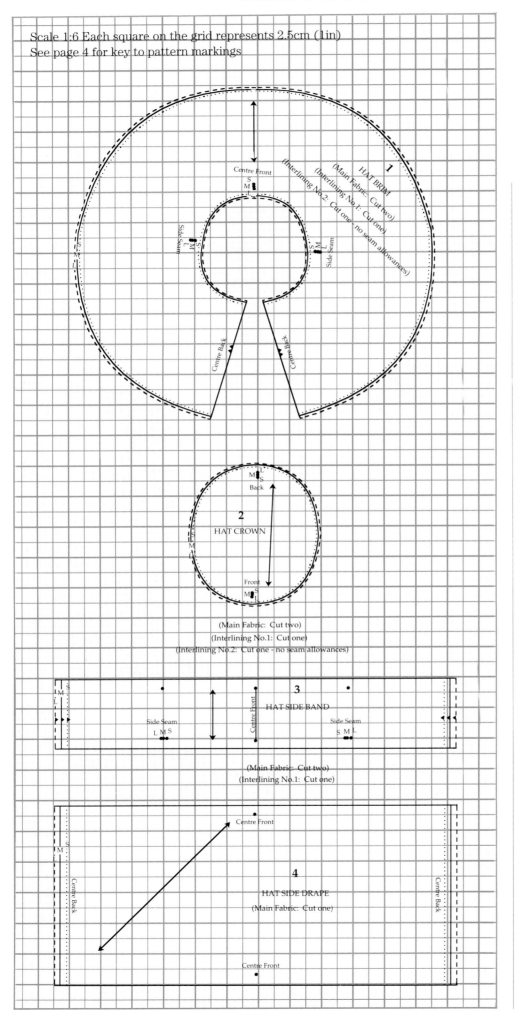

Scale 1:6 Each square on the grid represents 2.5cm (1in)
See page 4 for key to pattern markings

Centre Front

1

HAT BRIM

(Main Fabric: Cut two)
(Interlining No.1: Cut one)
(Interlining No.2: Cut one - no seam allowances)

Side Seam

Side Seam

Centre Back

Centre Back

Back

2

HAT CROWN

Front

(Main Fabric: Cut two)
(Interlining No.1: Cut one)
(Interlining No.2: Cut one - no seam allowances)

3

Centre Front

HAT SIDE BAND

Side Seam

Side Seam

(Main Fabric: Cut two)
(Interlining No.1: Cut one)

Centre Front

4

HAT SIDE DRAPE

(Main Fabric: Cut one)

Centre Back

Centre Back

Centre Front

----------- TIP -----------

Omit Step 7 if you want to save time. This is purely for decorative purposes.

FIG 2

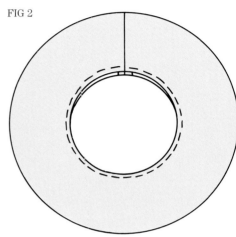

FIG 3

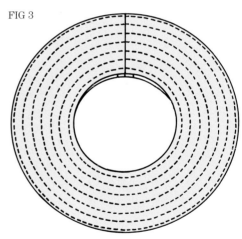

8. *Crown* Place canvas crown on top of Vilene crown. Machine 3mm ($\frac{1}{8}$in) inside the canvas edge. Place Vilene side down to the wrong side of the silk crown and machine 6mm ($\frac{1}{4}$in) outside the canvas.

9. Tack the Vilene to the first main fabric Side Band and machine the Centre Back seam. This will be known as the Main Side Band.

10. Machine Centre Back seam of the Side Drape. Press both seams open.

11. Lay the wrong side of the drape on top of the right side of the Main Side Band, matching up at Centre Back. Pin around the top and lower edge, machine 6mm ($\frac{1}{4}$in) from the edge.

Make this hat to match any casual outfit and you instantly create a designer look.

12. At the Centre Back evenly distribute the fullness of the drape over the back seam of the band. Pin and prickstitch in between the drapes to secure (*fig. 4*). Repeat at Centre Front and sides.

FIG 4

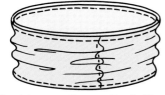

13. Matching up Centre Back, Front and Side •s, pin the draped band to the interlined crown (right sides together) at the top edge. Machine, taking usual seam allowance. Trim to 6mm (¼in), turn to right side and press. (A folded towel placed inside the crown may help in pressing the curved seam.)

14. Machine Centre Back seam of the second Side Band. Press open.

15. Matching up Centre Back, Front and Side •s, pin the crown which has not been interlined, to the band at the top edge. Machine and trim to 6mm (¼in). Turn to right side and press. This has formed the lining for the hat.

16. Place the lining inside the interlined crown, wrong sides together. Matching •s at the bottom, pin in place. Machine 6mm (¼in) in from the edge.

17. At the top of the crown secure the lining to the seam allowance of the main crown using a prickstitch.

18. *Putting Crown to Brim* Matching Centre Back and all •s, pin brim to the crown, right sides together. Machine usual seam allowance.

19. Place the curved petersham with the narrow edge down to the machine line. Starting at the Centre Back, edgestitch the petersham in place. Overlap the raw edge at the Centre Back. Hand stitch the overlap.

20. Turn to the wrong side of the petersham and trim 6mm (¼in) away from the seam. Clip remaining seam up to the stitching line all the way round.

Push petersham to the inside of the hat and bar tack down at the Centre Back.

21. *Appliquéd Flowers* The decoration on this hat is an arrangement of appliquéd flowers cut from the blouse fabric. Each flower is worked separately and hand stitched to the hat when complete.

APPLIQUÉ

1. Cut a square of fabric, incorporating the flower or design you wish to use for the appliqué. Now cut a square to the same size in each of the following: plain silk (for backing), firm interfacing (e.g. Vilene), and Bondaweb × 2.

2. Now adhere all layers together, following manufacturer's instructions for Bondaweb, in the following sequence: main fabric, Bondaweb,

Vilene, Bondaweb, silk backing. All layers have now become one.

3. Trim around the chosen shape.

4. Set your machine to a medium width, small length zigzag stitch. Starting at a corner if possible, stitch all around the raw edges. Stitch on and off the fabric to eliminate fraying and provide a firm finish.

If turning left around the corner of a design finish with the needle in the right position. If turning right, finish in the left position. This will avoid gaps in the stitching.

When you have completed all the appliquéd flowers, hand stitch to the hat in the required position. On the hat shown, I have stitched the flowers to the underside of the brim since the hat is worn with the brim turned up.

VALENTINO DRESS

I love the idea of mixing fabrics that would not usually be found together; not only different designs, such as spots, stripes, flowers and checks, but also different fabric weights, such as woollen tweeds teamed with lightweight silks.

The idea for the Valentino dress came when I visited one of my favourite fabric haunts. I proceeded to pull bolts of suitable fabric from the shelves in my quest to make a dress in black and white checked fabric with a contrasting multi-coloured bodice. Owner Barry was horrified but realized he had a would-be designer on his hands and

decided there was nothing to do except go along with the idea! Once we had selected every piece of black, white and flowered fabric available, I spotted it.

At the far end of the store a red and white checked woollen tweed caught my eye. In another distant corner was the red and white spotted silk crepe de chine, with that glorious black signature of Valentino.

I pulled them both out and declared 'This is it!'. Barry was delighted that no further chaos would ensue and smiled benignly. There was silence as he contemplated the fabrics until, at last, he spoke – 'Yes, I like it!'

MATERIALS REQUIRED

Bodice main fabric: size 10: 1.20m (1¹⁄₃yds) silk crepe de chine 115cm (44–45in) wide; size 12: 1.30m (1¹⁄₂yds); size 14: 1.40m (1⁵⁄₈yds)

Dress main fabric: size 10: 90cm (1yd) pure wool tweed 150cm (58–60in) wide; size 12: 1m (1¹⁄₈yds); size 14: 1m (1¹⁄₈yds)

Interlining No 1: size 10: 1.30m (1¹⁄₂yds) cotton mull 90cm (35–36in) wide; size 12: 1.40m (1¹⁄₂yds); size 14: 1.50m (1²⁄₃yds)

Interlining No 2: size 10: 2.70m (3yds) silk organza 108cm (43in) wide; size 12: 2.80m (3¹⁄₈yds); size 14: 2.90m (3¹⁄₈yds)

Lining: size 10: 2.40m (2²⁄₃yds) Habutai silk 90cm (35–36in) wide; size 12: 2.50m (2³⁄₄yds); size 14: 2.60m (2⁷⁄₈yds)

NOTIONS

5 covered buttons 3cm (1¹⁄₄in) diameter
25cm (10in) zip

─────────── TIP ───────────

If making this design in linen, cotton or silk, which would make a cool and elegant dress for the summer vacation; interline it with lining fabric such as Bremsilk and eliminate that extra lining layer. Do remember to neaten all inside seams in this case!

PATTERN PIECES

1 Front Bodice, 2 Back Bodice, 3 Sleeve, 4 Front Dress Panel, 5 Side Front Dress Panel, 6 Centre Back Dress Panel, 7 Side Back Dress Panel, 8 Front Neck Facing.
Lining Use 1–7 inclusive, referring to cutting lines for lining.

METHODS AND TECHNIQUES
INTERLINING AND REASONS WHY
SETTING IN SLEEVES
ZIP PLACEMENT
COVERED PRESS STUDS
LINING PLACEMENT
DARTS
SLEEVE HEADS
SHOULDER PADS

THE FABRICS

Main fabric Silk crepe de chine (bodice) and dress-weight, pure wool tweed.

Bodice Interlining No 1 Cotton mull was chosen for a number of reasons. We are going to work a lightweight silk with a tweed, so top priority is to bring the silk up in weight to be compatible with the wool. Cotton mull has a thickness to it, adding a richness and depth to the silk. The added density will prevent seam allowances and bulky ridges showing through the fine silk.

Bodice Interlining No 2 Silk organza will add the body lacking in the garment. Although pure silk organza is very light, it has more body than any other interlining. It has wonderful moulding qualities which will sculpture the bodice and sleeves beautifully.

Dress Interlining The tweed section of the garment does not require extra thickness but does need body. The tight weave of silk organza will complement

RIGHT: A unique combination of light silk and medium wool tweed, using interlinings for the silk to balance the fabric weights.

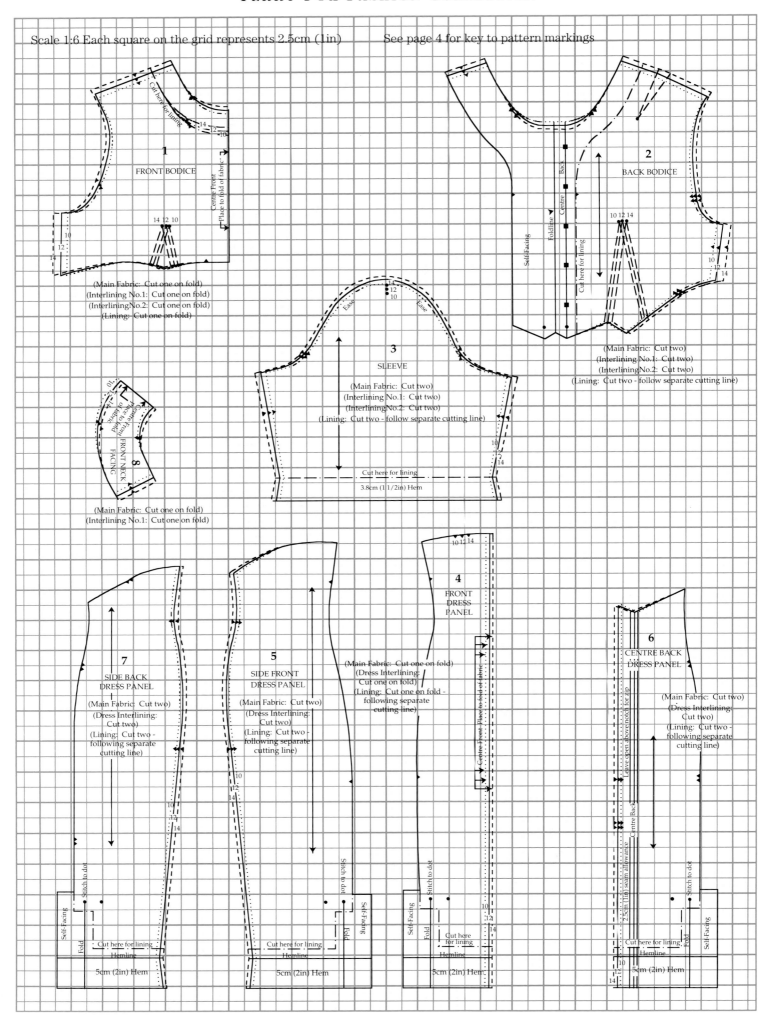

Scale 1:6 Each square on the grid represents 2.5cm (1in)   See page 4 for key to pattern markings

1
FRONT BODICE

14 12 10

14 12 10

Centre Front
Place to fold of fabric

Cut here for lining

(Main Fabric: Cut one on fold)
(Interlining No.1: Cut one on fold)
(InterliningNo.2: Cut one on fold)
(Lining: Cut one on fold)

2
BACK BODICE

Self-Facing   Foldline   Centre Back

Cut here for lining

10 12 14

10 12 14

(Main Fabric: Cut two)
(Interlining No.1: Cut two)
(InterliningNo.2: Cut two)
(Lining: Cut two - follow separate cutting line)

3
SLEEVE

Ease   Ease

14 12 10

(Main Fabric: Cut two)
(Interlining No.1: Cut two)
(InterliningNo.2: Cut two)
(Lining: Cut two - follow separate cutting line)

10
12
14

Cut here for lining
3.8cm (1 1/2in) Hem

8
FRONT NECK
FACING

Centre Front
Place to fold of fabric

(Main Fabric: Cut one on fold)
(Interlining No.1: Cut one on fold)

7
SIDE BACK
DRESS PANEL

(Main Fabric: Cut two)
(Dress Interlining:
Cut two)
(Lining: Cut two -
following separate
cutting line)

10
12
14

Self-Facing   Fold
Stitch to dot

Cut here for lining
Hemline
5cm (2in) Hem

5
SIDE FRONT
DRESS PANEL

(Main Fabric: Cut two)
(Dress Interlining:
Cut two)
(Lining: Cut two -
following separate
cutting line)

10
12
14

Fold   Self-Facing
Stitch to dot

Cut here for lining
Hemline
5cm (2in) Hem

4
FRONT
DRESS
PANEL

10 12 14

(Main Fabric: Cut one on fold)
(Dress Interlining:
Cut one on fold)
(Lining: Cut one on fold -
following separate
cutting line)

Centre Front. Place to fold of fabric

Self-Facing   Fold   Stitch to dot

10
12
14

Cut here
for lining
Hemline
5cm (2in) Hem

6
CENTRE BACK
DRESS PANEL

(Main Fabric: Cut two)
(Dress Interlining:
Cut two)
(Lining: Cut two -
following separate
cutting line)

Leave open above notch for zip

2.5cm (1in) seam allowance   Centre Back

Stitch to dot
Fold   Self-Facing

10
12
14

Cut here for lining
Hemline
5cm (2in) Hem

Use this technique for combining silk and wool to make a special coat or dress for a wedding. It's a great favourite with couture designers.

the more open tweed weave and prevent seating.
Lining Habutai silk – a natural fabric, light and cool.

METHOD
BODICE
1. Cut pattern pieces 1, 2 and 3 in main fabric, lining, interlining no 1 and 2. Cut piece 8 in main fabric and interlining no 1. Iron all corresponding pieces together, in that order. Pin together to prevent movement then tack all layers together 13mm (½in) from the raw edge, ensuring all layers are absolutely flat to each other. Now treat as one layer.
2. Make darts (Couture Techniques) in Front and Back, press towards centre.
3. Next fold the bodice facing back on the foldline and press lightly. Turn to the wrong side and open out facing. Trim the organza interlining to 13mm (½in) from the foldline on the facing side.

───────── TIP ─────────

Whenever working with interfacing or interlinings which need to be cut away, always cut the interfacing 13mm (½in) beyond the foldline. In this way the outer edge of the interfacing cannot distort the finished foldline if not cut absolutely straight. In addition, the strong fibres of the interfacing will wear the garment from the inside outwards.

───────────────────────

4. Blindstitch on the foldline of the organza (through the cotton mull and main fabric) to secure in place. Only a tiny stitch should show on the right side of the garment in the foldline. This will be invisible when turned back.
5. Machine bodice Front to bodice Back at shoulder seams and side seams.
6. Machine stitch side seams of sleeves. Clip seam at hemline of sleeve.
7. Machine Back and Front facing together at shoulder seams.
8. Using the 3-Point Press (Couture Techniques), open all seams.
9. With right sides together, lay facing around the neckline, matching •s. Machine, taking 15mm (⅝in) seam

*BELOW AND RIGHT: Extra care taken to match checks and
stripes at the seams is the hallmark of a couture finish.*

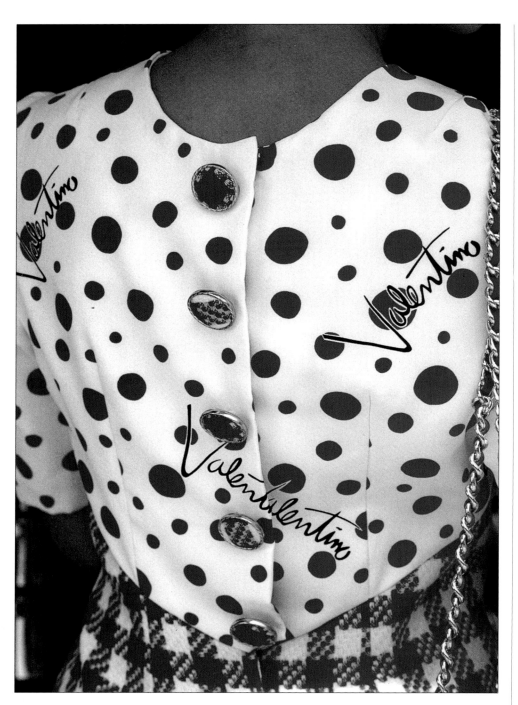

12. Now machine a straight line 6mm
(¼in) in from the raw edge of the sleeve
hem, keeping all layers together.
Do the same for the facing edge.
13. Turn up the required hemline of
sleeve and blindstitch to the organza
interlining.
14. Cut out and then machine all lining
bodice pieces together to the same
stage. Press seams open and darts to
the centre.
15. Press in the seam allowances at the
sleeve hemline, Centre Back, Front and
Back neck edges. (You will need to clip
around the curve.) With right sides
together, match the lining to the neck
edge, having seam lines matching. Pin
and slipstitch in place.
16. Position the hem edge of the sleeve
lining against the top of the sleeve hem.
Slipstitch in place. Lightly press all
stitching.
17. Secure the neck facing to the
shoulder pad at the shoulder seam with
a bar tack.

MAIN SKIRT OF DRESS
18. Cut pattern pieces 4, 5, 6 and 7 in
main fabric, lining and dress interlining.
Matching Up Checks Cut each panel
individually, starting with the Centre
Front panel.
    Take the Side panel and line up with
the Centre Front at waist level so that
checks around the body are even (you
will need to adjust the pattern position
on the fabric until they line up). Then
line up the Side panel to the Front
panel at the seam line to ensure the
checks are in line lengthways. Do this
by folding back the seam allowance so
that you can see what the finished
effect will be. Turn back the Side panel
at the seam allowance. This should
show the next check, e.g. if the Front
panel shows red, the Side panel should
show white. Cut out the Side panel

—————————— TIP ——————————
I recommend the use of a walking foot
when machining check fabrics. This will
prevent slippage between layers,
keeping checks in line.

allowance. Trim away the corner and
layer seams. Clip up to the stitching all
around neck edge. Press. Turn to the
right side and press again, rolling the
seam line slightly to the inside.
Prickstitch around the neckline, but do
not go through to the main fabric.
10. *Centre Back Opening* Turn the
facing back at the lower Centre Back so

that right sides are together. Machine
from the foldline (small ●) to the large
●, 15mm (⅝in) in from raw edge. Trim
corner, layer seam. Clip to the large ●
and turn to right side, press.
11. Complete the sleeves following the
Couture Techniques for setting-in,
sleeve heads and shoulder pads (pages
119 to 120).

LEFT AND RIGHT: Extend the hemline to ankle length and match the dress with a bolero jacket for a stylish evening outfit.

when you are happy with the position.
    Repeat the technique for Back and Centre Back panels.
19. Press corresponding interlining pieces to wrong side of main fabric and tack 13mm (¹/₂in) from the edges. Treat as one layer.
20. Machine Side Back panels to Centre Back from top edge down to large •.
21. Machine Centre Back seam from zip notch downwards.
22. Join Front Side panels to Centre Front panel from top edge down to large •. Machine. The area from • to hemline will form the hemline vents. Clip the seams and press open using the 3-Point Press.

FIG 1

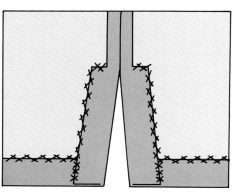

23. Place the zip in the Centre Back using the Couture Technique, page 121 (omitting stage 6 for this garment.)
24. Machine side seams together, clip and press open.
25. Now pin the bodice to the skirt, matching all seam and dart lines. Machine and press the seam, ironing upwards to the bodice.
26. Turn up the required hem amount. Turn back the vent facings to the wrong side, along the foldline. Press. Using a cross stitch, secure the raw edge of the facing where it sits upon the hem.
27. Using a herringbone stitch, secure the hem and facings back to the organza (*fig.1*).

FIG 2

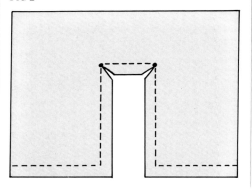

28. Machine all remaining lining pieces together. Clip and press open seams. For hem vents snip into the corners at the top of each vent. Press the seam allowance to the wrong side all the way round the vent and hemline (*fig.2*).
29. With wrong sides together and seam lines matching, pin the lining to the dress hemline. Position so that the lining seam line lies 15mm (⁵/₈in) from the herringboned hem facing and vent edges (*fig.3*). Slipstitch the lining in place.
30. Take the lining up to meet the bodice and lay flat over the upward facing seam into the bodice. Turn in the lining around the zip and slipstitch around the zip. Tack along the top seam at midriff level.
31. Now bring the bodice lining down, clipping to ease into the curve. Turn under 15mm (⁵/₈in) all the way round and place over the main dress lining. Pin and slipstitch in place at the midriff seam line. Stitch through the lining to seam allowance and secure.
32. *Button Fastening* Lay the left bodice Back over the right. Position the five buttons evenly along the left side on the Centre Back edge. Attach to the dress, stitching through to the facing.
33. Turn over to the facing on the inside and stitch five covered press studs (Couture Techniques) on top of the stitching which corresponds to each button.
34. Overlap the bodice panels again, and stitch the other half of the covered press studs in place. Finish with a hook on the left facing and a bar tack on the right bodice Back (right side of fabric).

FIG 3

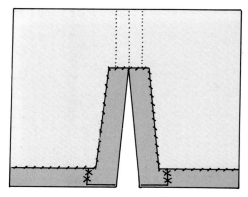

IVY LEAF DRESS

*I*n many ways garments are very much like people. Each has its own special characteristic; it may be dramatic styling, a sense of humour or simple elegance. The Ivy Leaf Dress, to me, is a very feminine garment.

I designed it for a garden party or similar daytime occasion; hence the use of pale green embroidery incorporating a trellis and leaf design. However, with the right accessories, it could easily be a stunning alternative to the more traditional long bridal gown.

With the basic design and event in mind, I began to experiment with embellishment ideas. I made up various small sample pieces of appliqué, pin-tucking, quilting with baby ribbon and shadow work, a technique which is explained in full on page 118. I played for hours with machine and hand embroidery. As you can imagine, one idea can quickly lead to more. Soon a three-dimensional effect came to the fore, with the idea of placing potpourri in the cup-shaped pockets around the hem. Thinking it through I realized that it wasn't entirely practical; so I turned to my 'inspiration' box which is full of odd buttons, beads, sequins and diamantes. Any of these items would work in the pockets but I eventually decided on the tiny peach and cream beads; they looked so feminine.

Thus the design came first with this dress; the fabrics, decoration and methods came later. All the time spent experimenting will not be wasted; those ideas are locked away until the right fabric and style provides the key to release them!

MATERIALS REQUIRED (SIZES 10–14)

Check fabric requirements if you select narrower fabrics than those detailed.

Main fabric: 9.50m (10¹/₃yds) pure silk organza 109cm (43in) wide
Underlayer: 3.10m (3¹/₃yds) Thai silk taffeta 112cm 44in) wide
Interlining: 1.50m (1²/₃yds) Tie interlining 94cm (37in) wide
Lining: 1m (1¹/₈yds) Bremsilk 140cm (52–54in) wide

——————— TIP ———————

Economize on fabric and time by omitting the shadow work. Thus, you will only require three layers of organza instead of four.

As an alternative to organza, use a denser fabric, such as dupion or taffeta and a contrasting colour for the piping. In this case, you will not require the underlayer of fabric.

NOTIONS

35cm (¹/₃yd) pale green lightweight fabric for piping (e.g. crepe de chine or lining)
50cm (20in) zip
130m (142yds) pale green Madeira four-strand pure silk embroidery floss (No 1309)
Beads in peach and cream (quantity will

LEFT: This dress gives me great pleasure just playing with the beads between the two layers of fabric.

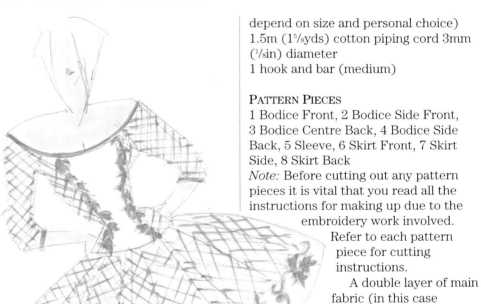

depend on size and personal choice)
1.5m (1⁵/₈yds) cotton piping cord 3mm (¹/₈in) diameter
1 hook and bar (medium)

PATTERN PIECES

1 Bodice Front, 2 Bodice Side Front, 3 Bodice Centre Back, 4 Bodice Side Back, 5 Sleeve, 6 Skirt Front, 7 Skirt Side, 8 Skirt Back
Note: Before cutting out any pattern pieces it is vital that you read all the instructions for making up due to the embroidery work involved.
Refer to each pattern piece for cutting instructions.
A double layer of main fabric (in this case organza) is required for the Shadow Work. We also use two layers elsewhere to

METHODS AND TECHNIQUES

INTERLINING AND REASONS WHY
EMBROIDERY WITH SHADOW WORK
SET-IN SLEEVES
BEAD POCKETS
ZIP PLACEMENT
BABY MACHINED HEM
HONG KONG FINISH
FRENCH SEAM
HAIRLINE FRENCH SEAM
COVERED HOOK AND BAR
COVERED PIPING CORD
ROULEAUX LOOPS

Scale 1:6 Each square on the grid represents 2.5cm (1in)   See page 4 for key to pattern markings

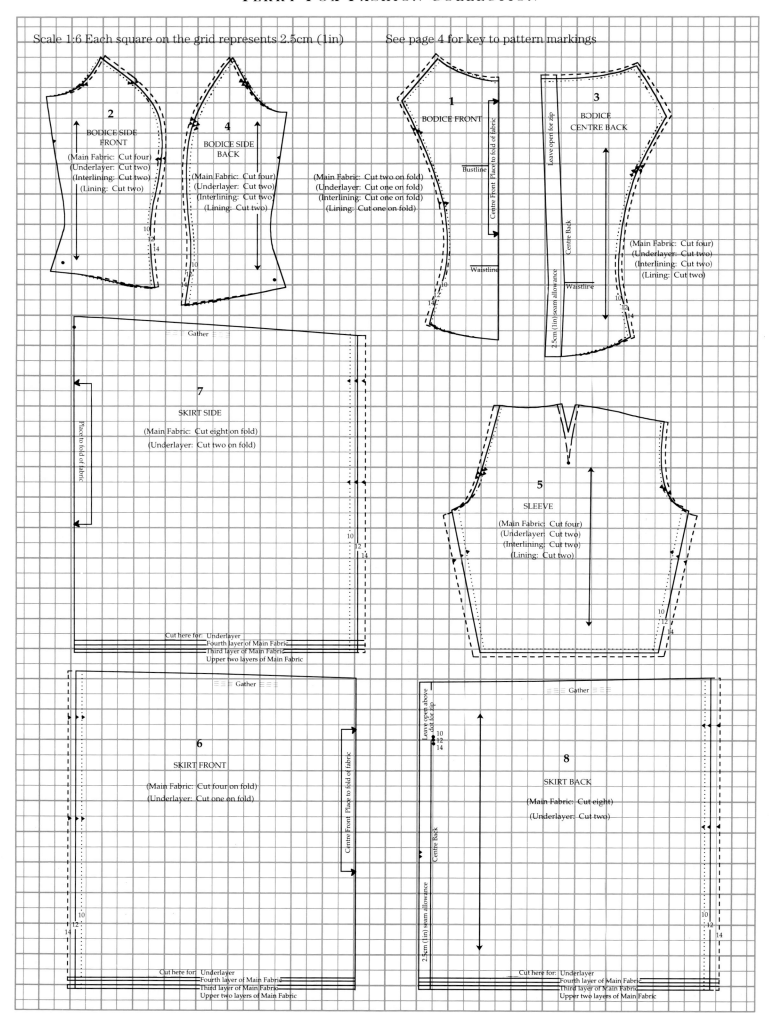

2
BODICE SIDE
FRONT
(Main Fabric: Cut four)
(Underlayer: Cut two)
(Interlining: Cut two)
(Lining: Cut two)

10
12
14

4
BODICE SIDE
BACK
(Main Fabric: Cut four)
(Underlayer: Cut two)
(Interlining: Cut two)
(Lining: Cut two)

10
12
14

1
BODICE FRONT
Bustline
Waistline
Centre Front Place to fold of fabric
(Main Fabric: Cut two on fold)
(Underlayer: Cut one on fold)
(Interlining: Cut one on fold)
(Lining: Cut one on fold)

10
12
14

3
BODICE
CENTRE BACK
Leave open for zip
Centre Back
2.5cm (1in) seam allowance
Waistline
(Main Fabric: Cut four)
(Underlayer: Cut two)
(Interlining: Cut two)
(Lining: Cut two)

10
12
14

7
SKIRT SIDE
(Main Fabric: Cut eight on fold)
(Underlayer: Cut two on fold)
Gather
Place to fold of fabric

10
12
14

Cut here for: Underlayer
Fourth layer of Main Fabric
Third layer of Main Fabric
Upper two layers of Main Fabric

5
SLEEVE
(Main Fabric: Cut four)
(Underlayer: Cut two)
(Interlining: Cut two)
(Lining: Cut two)

10
12
14

6
SKIRT FRONT
(Main Fabric: Cut four on fold)
(Underlayer: Cut one on fold)
Gather
Centre Front Place to fold of fabric

10
12
14

Cut here for: Underlayer
Fourth layer of Main Fabric
Third layer of Main Fabric
Upper two layers of Main Fabric

8
SKIRT BACK
(Main Fabric: Cut eight)
(Underlayer: Cut two)
Gather
Leave open above dot for zip
Centre Back
2.5cm (1in) seam allowance

10
12
14

10
12
14

Cut here for: Underlayer
Fourth layer of Main Fabric
Third layer of Main Fabric
Upper two layers of Main Fabric

Guaranteed to strike up a conversation, the beaded shadow work can be applied to absolutely anything from wedding gowns to little girls' dresses – children love it!

be consistent throughout the dress. However, if you wish to use a denser fabric and omit the Shadow Work, only one layer will be necessary. Remember to adjust your fabric purchase as appropriate.

Note: Pattern pieces 2, 4, 5, 6, 7 and 8 which will be embroidered, should be cut individually, following steps 1 and 2, Bodice Method.

THE FABRICS

Main fabric Pure silk organza has a very delicate appearance, particularly in the shade I have chosen. Unlike chiffon, organza is very firm with lots of body and bounce; a perfect choice for this type of frothy skirt.

One of the Couture Techniques used on this dress is Shadow Work (page 118), which will always require two layers of sheer fabric. A shading effect is formed by cutting away various sections of the lower layer of sheer fabric. As the fabric density changes so will the colour, producing the shadow effect.

Underlayer The organza needs added density to prevent it being transparent. A light ivory layer of Thai silk taffeta under the four layers of organza will provide this. Thai silk taffeta is usually less expensive, with a lighter handle than ordinary taffeta and will complement the layers with its firm handle and frothy nature.

Interlining Tie interlining is firm and holds its shape well. As the name suggests, it is more usual to find it in a tie, but I found it ideal for interlining the dress bodice, since it is neither too thick nor too hard.

Lining This dress is intended to be light and I did not, therefore, want to add unnecessary bulk. Bremsilk is a light fabric and breathes well, making it suitable for lining the fitted bodice. The skirt is only lined with taffeta (see Underlayer above).

METHOD
BODICE
All bodice and sleeve embroidery should be completed before making up the bodice. Remember that you will cut two layers of each pattern piece in organza.

First, mark the trellis embroidery design; the easiest way to work evenly and accurately is to work in a square. Follow the method below for each pattern piece you are going to embroider.

1. Take each pattern piece separately and cut two organza squares large enough for the pattern. Tack around the edges to keep the two squares together. Lay the squares on a flat surface and place the paper pattern in the middle. You must be very accurate in matching the middle point of the pattern with the middle point of the squares.

────────── TIP ──────────

If you are going to machine embroider the trellis design, have the wrong side of the fabric uppermost.

────────────────────────

2. Draw around the pattern piece using a light pencil. Remove the pattern. Now draw diagonal lines to each corner of the squares. These are your guidelines. From these lines you can draw parallel lines which are exactly 2.5cm (1in) apart over the entire pattern outline (*fig. 1*). These are the lines along which you will embroider, either by machine or by hand.

By hand: Using two strands of the green embroidery thread and an

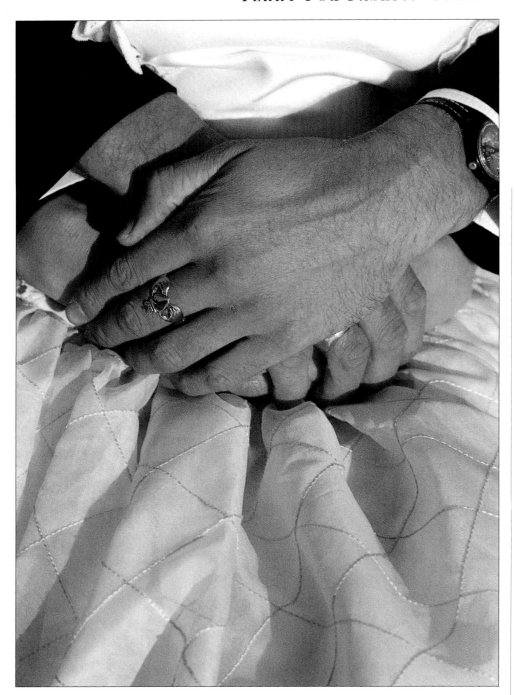

LEFT AND RIGHT: This pattern with short or long skirt would make a lovely wedding dress and, as practicality would not be so important, the little pockets could be filled with rose petals.

embroidery needle, stitch along all lines using a small, continuous backstitch.
By machine: Wind the embroidery thread (two strands) around the bobbin

FIG 1

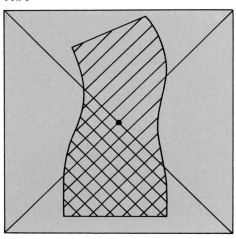

making sure that you have sufficient thread to complete a line. Be firm when winding on but not too tight. Use an ivory top thread (for example Gütermann polyester) and set your machine to a medium-size, straight stitch with a loose tension. Test the stitch on a fabric scrap first.

Place the two layers under the machine with the wrong side uppermost. Machine a straight row following the pencil line. Take it slowly as you will be stitching across the bias of the fabric, be careful not to stretch the material.

Complete all embroidered bodice pieces and sleeves in this manner and then continue as below.

3. All bodice panels and sleeves comprise two layers of organza, even

if they are not embroidered. Take the two layers of organza for each panel and sleeve, add one layer of taffeta, then one layer of interlining. Lightly press all four layers together. Now tack around the outer edge, using Kinkame thread, to secure them as one layer.

4. Join the Side Fronts to Centre Front; Side Backs to Centre Back. Machine the sleeve darts and sleeve seams. Clip all seams and press open.

5. Take the Centre Backs and press along the foldlines, turning the allowances to the wrong side. Remember that there will be a 2.5cm (1in) allowance for the zip.

6. Insert the zip following the instructions in the Couture Techniques (page 121). Leave 5cm (2in) of the zip free at the bottom of the bodice, this will be attached to the skirt. Do not prickstitch the zip in place until the piping cord has been placed around the neckline.

7. Machine the bodice side seams, joining Back and Front sections. Clip and press open the seams.

8. Set-in the sleeves matching the •s at front and back, and the underarm seamlines. Machine the full seam allowance. Strengthen the underarm area between the front and back •s by machining a second row 6mm (¹/₄in) from the first line but in the seam allowance. Trim up to the second stitching line. For guidance, see Couture Technique page 119.

9. *Piping.* Cut a length of piping cord to go around the entire neckline and the hemlines of both sleeves. Cover this cord following the Couture Technique on page 116.

Use the pale green fabric to line the cord and the organza as the outer layer so that the piping matches the embroidery.

10. Place the covered cord around the neckline and sleeve edge, to the left of the seam line. At the sleeve edge you will have to overlap the cord at the seam to conceal the raw end. Tuck in the covered cord at the Centre Back foldline (*fig.2*). Machine in place 1.5mm (¹/₁₆in) from the edge of the

BORDER EMBROIDERY DESIGN: Shown half size in two halves. Each square on the grid represents 1cm (⅜in). To enlarge, see page 8. The dotted lines show how the two halves fit together. Transfer the design to the dress, starting at the Centre Front, repeating the whole design four times around the hemline. For larger dress sizes, elongate the design slightly.

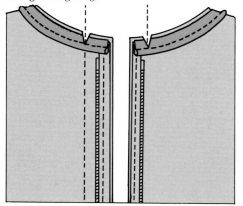

FIG 2

cord. Now fold back the allowance at the Centre Back foldline and prickstitch the zip in place.

11. Make up the bodice lining to the same stage, clipping and pressing all seams open.

12. With right sides together, pin the lining to the bodice all around the neckline, starting and finishing at the Centre Back. Using a zip foot on your machine, stitch the lining to the bodice. Stitch as close as possible to the covered cord.

13. Clip through all thicknesses of the seam allowance, up to the cord. With a Straw needle and double thread overstitch the seam allowance (including the lining) to the interlining. Turn the lining to the right side.

14. Stitch the covered cord to the sleeve edge before bringing the lining down. Clip up to the cord and overstitch the seam allowance down to the interlining. Now bring the sleeve lining down, matching up seamlines. Clip around the lining hem, up to the 15mm (⅝in) allowance. Turn under the allowance and slipstitch to sleeve edge, concealing the seam allowance.

15. Turn under the lining allowance all the way round the zip and pin in place.

LEFT: The shadow work technique has endless possibilities. It could be used to make a very delicate Christening gown or, on a larger scale, embroidered on white or cream voile, to create beautiful, sheer window drapes.

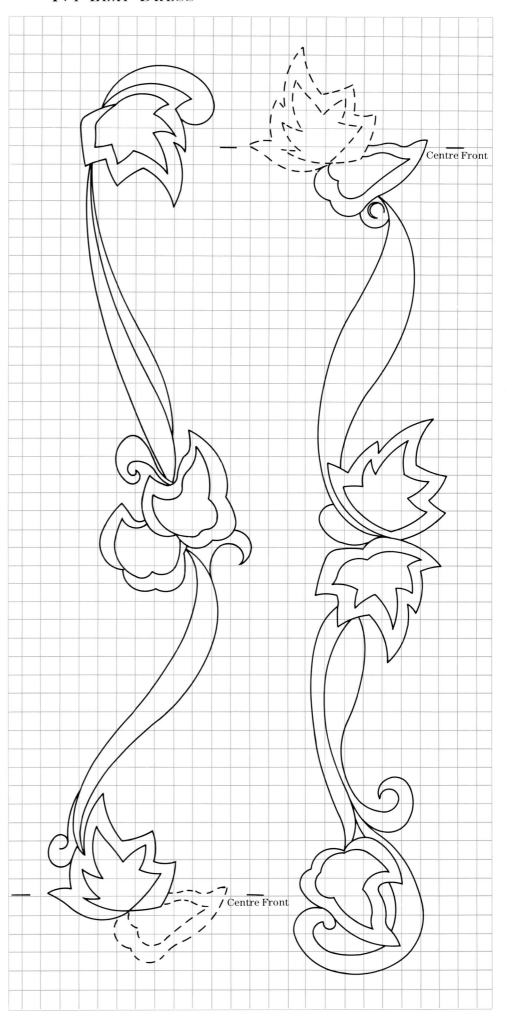

Centre Front

Centre Front

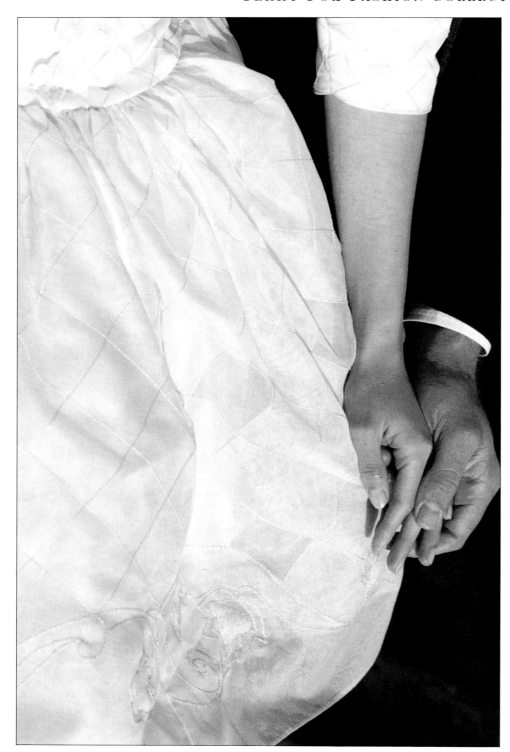

LEFT: A close up of the beaded leaves. RIGHT: A full view of how the piping sits round the neckline. Two elegant embellishments which enhance the design without overpowering it.

Draw in the trellis lines above the border design, having the lines 5cm (2in) apart. Cover the skirt completely, checking that the trellis lines will meet up at the Centre Back seam.

5. Complete the border embroidery and bead pockets before the trellis stitching. I recommend you work this entirely by hand; it is so much easier to stitch the curves and to fill the pockets with beads.

6. Now complete the embroidery for the trellis, either by machine or hand. Machine embroidery is obviously quicker but remember you will have to work on the wrong side.

When the design is completely finished, trim the Centre Back seam to 15mm ($^5/_8$in) from the • downwards. Join this section by French seam.

7. Trim the seam allowance from • upwards to 6mm ($^1/_4$in) and neaten the opening with a Hong Kong finish (Couture Techniques page 115).

8. Machine the main fabric hem using the Baby Machined Hem technique on page 114. All tacking used to hold the two organza layers together should have been removed by now.

9. Now take the second two layers of organza (remember you have cut four layers of organza for the skirt). Working in single layers this time, join all seams together using a Hairline French seam (page 114). The Centre Back seam should only be joined from • downwards. Trim the seam allowance above this point to 6mm ($^1/_4$in).

10. Turn under the hem 3mm ($^1/_8$in) and press. Turn under a further 3mm ($^1/_8$in) and machine. Don't machine each turning as you will have two rows of stitching showing when only one is required. Repeat for second layer.

11. Now place one layer on top of the other, wrong side to right side. Tack together around the Centre Back opening and then join the two together with a Hong Kong finish at this opening. This eliminates the extra bulk of two finishes.

12. *Taffeta Underlayer* Join all seams together using a French Seam, leaving the Centre Back open from the •

SKIRT

1. Remember to cut four layers of organza for the skirt; two of which will form the main fabric layer. For easier handling I recommend you tack the first two layers together (i.e. main fabric layer), using Kinkame thread and a Straw needle. The second two layers will be handled as single layers.

2. Using a French seam (Couture Techniques) join all seams together except the Centre Back.

3. Tack a line 2.5cm (1in) in from the raw edges at the Centre Back. Using a light pencil line transfer the border design from the chart to the skirt

hemline. Position it approximately 7.5cm (3in) up from the raw edge, ensuring that the pattern will match at the finished Centre Back seam. If necessary, elongate the design slightly to make it fit the fabric area.

4. We now need to mark out the trellis design on the skirt, as we did for the bodice and sleeves, using the top two layers of organza only. Refer to the Couture Techniques section on Shadow Work for marking out the Centre Front square which will act as your guideline. Remember to draw the lines on the wrong side of the skirt if you are going to machine embroider the trellis design.

*A close view of the trellis design on the bodice and the
leaves filled with beads which are held in position by
the backstitched veins.*

84

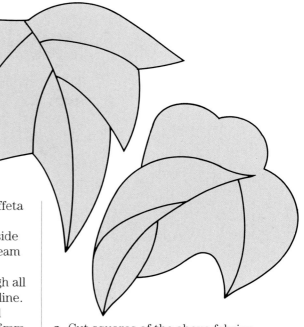

Bodice Front Leaf Appliqué Templates: Shown actual size. Use the two different templates for variety. Work the leaf veins in backstitch using embroidery floss.

upwards. Do not trim. Finish the lower raw edge with a Baby Machined Hem.

13. Gather the top edge of the main skirt (see tip below).

Place the skirt to the bodice, right sides together and matching skirt opening to Centre Back foldline of the bodice, side seams and Centre Front. Pull the gathers to fit and machine the usual seam allowance.

Gather the top of the next two layers of organza individually. Place them to the main skirt, matching up seamlines etc. as above. Pull up the gathers of the first layer, pin in place. Pull up the gathers of the second layer and pin. Machine through both layers at the same time.

––––––––––––––– TIP ––––––––––––––

To achieve evenly-spaced gathering always use three rows of stitching. The needlepoint will mark this fine fabric so keep all gathering lines within the seam allowance. I use a large, loose machine stitch for speed. Pull up all the threads together to ensure gathers are more evenly spaced.

––––––––––––––––––––––––––––––––––

14. Now place the taffeta skirt to the bodice. The sequence of layers should be: right side of main skirt to right side

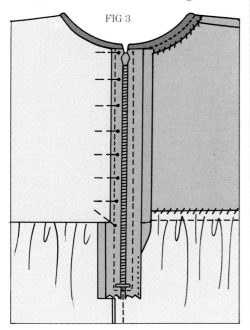

FIG 3

of bodice, two layers of organza, taffeta skirt with wrong side uppermost.

Match up the Centre Front and side seams. Open up the Centre Back seam allowance of the bodice and skirt, matching foldlines. Machine through all layers along the 15mm (⁵⁄₈in) seamline.

15. Stitch a second row through all layers of the seam, approximately 6mm (¹⁄₄in) from the first (within the seam allowance). Trim the excess and with a medium size zigzag, overstitch the edge to flatten the bulk.

16. Lay the waist seam up towards the bodice. Open up the Centre Back seam and complete the zip placement, starting with the Right side. The zip will be fixed to the taffeta layer only. Prickstitch in place. Turn any excess taffeta in the Centre Back allowance to the wrong side of the zip and prickstitch in place (*fig.3*).

17. Secure the seam allowance along the waistline through all thicknesses by oversewing down to the interlining and up both Centre Back seam allowances of the zip, taking the strain off the prickstitching.

Continue to place the bodice lining around the zip and the waistline by turning under the seam allowance.

Slipstitch in place.

18. Prickstitch around the neckline, approximately 6mm (¹⁄₄in) from the piped edge. Stitch through to the seam allowance only. This will prevent the lining from rolling towards the front.

FINISHING TOUCHES

19. Complete the bodice embellishment with a row of ivy leaves stitched to either side of the bustline. I attached sixteen leaves (eight either side).
You will need:
• Small pieces of tie interlining, taffeta and organza
• Ivy leaf templates
• Flexible drinking straw
• Cream and peach beads, as used for the bead pockets
• Embroidery needle
• Madeira embroidery floss as before
• Straw needle
• Ivory polyester thread

a. Cut squares of the above fabrics slightly larger than the leaf template. Cut the following for each leaf and lay them on top of each other; 1 × interlining, 1 × taffeta, 2 × organza. Use both templates for leaf variety.

b. Place a pin in the middle to keep all layers together then transfer the leaf outline to the fabric using a light pencil line.

c. Set your machine to a medium width, close zigzag stitch. Starting at the centre top of the leaf, machine just inside the pencil outline and stop about 13mm (¹⁄₂in) from the start point. Keeping the fabric under the machine, use the drinking straw to push and blow the beads into the leaf between the taffeta and double organza layers. I used about 100 very tiny beads for each leaf.

Remove the straw and complete the machine zigzag to the starting point.

d. Using a very sharp pair of small scissors trim the fabric around the leaf shape, as close as possible to the stitching line.

e. Using the embroidery floss (two strands) and needle, work a line of backstitch through the middle of the leaf from top to bottom to define the leaf vein. You may wish to embroider more veins.

f. Use the Straw needle and double polyester thread to prickstitch each leaf in position on the bustline.

20. Cover a medium-sized hook and bar (Couture Techniques page 112) and hand stitch in place at the inside top of the dress.

21. Make two hanging loops for the dress (Couture Techniques – Rouleaux Loops) from lining scraps. Stitch these loops to the bodice side seams. The folded length of the loops should be approximately 32cm (13in).

A BEAUTIFUL PINK BALLGOWN

Creating a design, or even choosing a pattern, for a special occasion can be a puzzle. We look all around us for ideas, perhaps turning to books or magazines; I often look to nature for inspiration. Many ideas will float to the surface but you can guarantee that whatever the theme, no two people will have exactly the same thoughts or views.

When I decided upon a pink ballgown, pretty pink shells jumped to mind. So to the shell store I went; such a variety of large and small, three-dimensional effects. I was fascinated by the lines across the shell and wondered how I could achieve the same effect with fabric. I had now started to create an atmosphere, a mood for my dress. The shells had conjured up sea breezes. Floating and rippling in these breezes were lengths of beautiful silk chiffon – perfect for my shells.

However, I couldn't see myself in a dress completely made of chiffon, preferring a more sculptured shape overall since I'm quite short and a little round in places – or should I say curvy! A mass of voluminous chiffon would not be at all flattering for me.

So let's see, what's available and more importantly, what will complement the chiffon? The gown has to be classical, timeless, yet stunningly styled to current fashion trends. A tall order, but not an unusual one! A browse through magazines will tell me what fabrics are popular. Dupion, taffeta, satin. . . . Duchesse satin. There's an idea! I rushed to my favourite fabric store. There it

was, just waiting for me, the perfect pink satin. The ideal combination is found; a gown incorporating the contrast of a deep, rich Duchesse satin against a delicately ruched, pure silk chiffon.

I almost feel that I have cheated with this design. The end result seems to have come from nowhere, purely from allowing my imagination to float, feeling the occasion. Ultimately, the process was one of elimination and luck. The fabrics, however, are deliberate choices to satisfy the required end result. It is important to give a lot of thought to your choice of pattern, fabrics and finishes. Keep in mind your budget, figure shape and personality, the time of year and the event.

The thought of all the fine ruching on this gown can be quite formidable but the finished effect is more than worth the time and care.

MATERIALS REQUIRED (SIZES 10–14)

Fabric requirements will be the same for all sizes as wide fabrics are used. *Note:* It will not be possible to purchase lining material in a suitable width for this garment. The lining will have to be joined before cutting out the pattern.

MAIN DRESS

Main fabric: 5.10m (5½yds) Duchesse satin 140cm (52–54in) wide
Bodice interlining No 1: 1m (1⅛yds) domette 90cm (36in) wide
Bodice interlining No 2: 1m (1⅛yds) cotton lawn 90cm (36in) wide
Bodice interlining No 3: 1m (1⅛yds) muslin 90cm (35–36in) wide
Bodice interlining No 4: 1m (1⅛yds) firm collar and cuff canvas 93cm (37in) wide
Bodice ruching: 4m (4⅜yds) chiffon 115cm (44–45in) wide

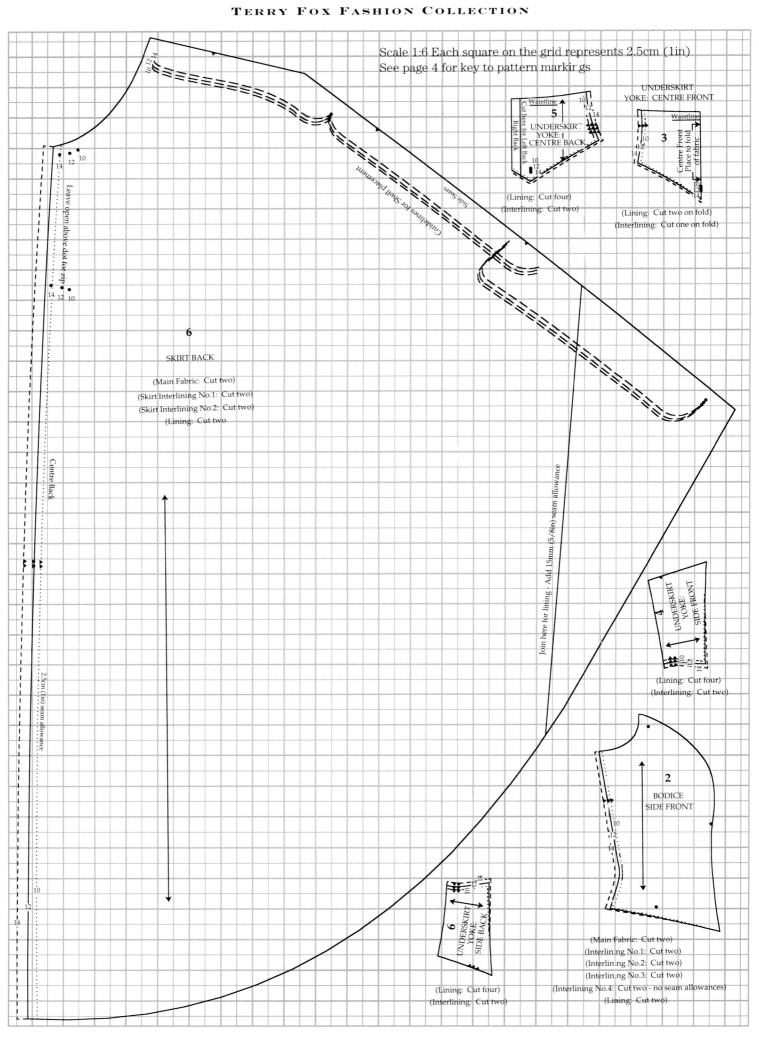

Scale 1:6 Each square on the grid represents 2.5cm (1in)
See page 4 for key to pattern markings

10 12 14

UNDERSKIRT
YOKE: CENTRE FRONT

Waistline

5

UNDERSKIRT
YOKE: CENTRE BACK

Cut here for Left Back
Right Back

Waistline

10
12
14

3

Centre Front
Place to fold
of fabric

10
12
14

10
12
14

(Lining: Cut four)

(Interlining: Cut two)

(Lining: Cut two on fold)

(Interlining: Cut one on fold)

Leave open above dot for zip

12 10

14

Guidelines for Shell placement

Side seam

Side seam

14 12 10

6

SKIRT BACK

(Main Fabric: Cut two)

(Skirt Interlining No.1: Cut two)

(Skirt Interlining No.2: Cut two)

(Lining: Cut two)

Centre Back

Join here for lining - Add 15mm (5/8in) seam allowance

UNDERSKIRT
YOKE:
SIDE FRONT

4

10
12
14

(Lining: Cut four)

(Interlining: Cut two)

2

BODICE
SIDE FRONT

10
12
14

2.5cm (1in) seam allowance

10

12

14

UNDERSKIRT
YOKE:
SIDE BACK

6

10 12 14

(Main Fabric: Cut two)

(Interlining No.1: Cut two)

(Interlining No.2: Cut two)

(Interlining No.3: Cut two)

(Interlining No.4: Cut two - no seam allowances)

(Lining: Cut two)

(Lining: Cut four)

(Interlining: Cut two)

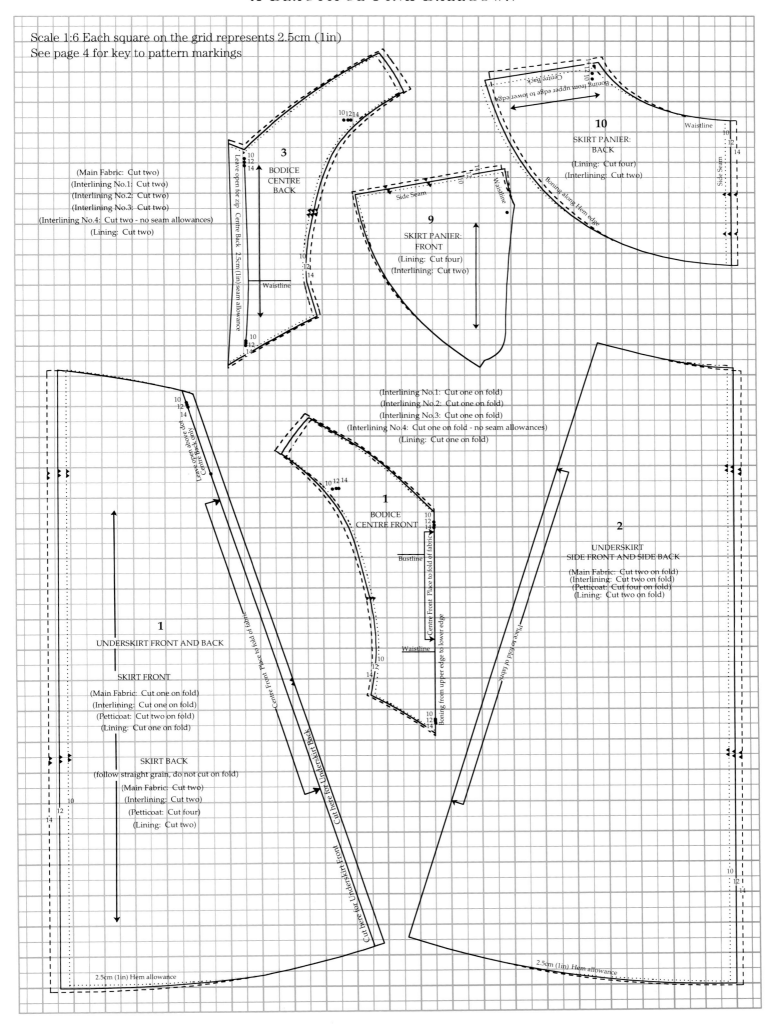

Scale 1:6 Each square on the grid represents 2.5cm (1in)
See page 4 for key to pattern markings

3
BODICE
CENTRE
BACK

(Main Fabric: Cut two)
(Interlining No.1: Cut two)
(Interlining No.2: Cut two)
(Interlining No.3: Cut two)
(Interlining No.4: Cut two - no seam allowances)
(Lining: Cut two)

Leave open for zip Centre Back 2.5cm (1in) seam allowance
Waistline

10
SKIRT PANIER:
BACK
(Lining: Cut four)
(Interlining: Cut two)
Centre Back
Boning from upper edge to lower edge
Boning along Hem edge
Waistline
Side Seam

9
SKIRT PANIER:
FRONT
(Lining: Cut four)
(Interlining: Cut two)
Side Seam
Waistline

(Interlining No.1: Cut one on fold)
(Interlining No.2: Cut one on fold)
(Interlining No.3: Cut one on fold)
(Interlining No.4: Cut one on fold - no seam allowances)
(Lining: Cut one on fold)

1
BODICE
CENTRE FRONT
Bustline
Centre Front Place to fold of fabric
Centre Front Place to fold of fabric
Boning from upper edge to lower edge
Waistline

2
UNDERSKIRT
SIDE FRONT AND SIDE BACK
(Main Fabric: Cut two on fold)
(Interlining: Cut two on fold)
(Petticoat: Cut four on fold)
(Lining: Cut two on fold)
Place to fold of fabric

1
UNDERSKIRT FRONT AND BACK

SKIRT FRONT
(Main Fabric: Cut one on fold)
(Interlining: Cut one on fold)
(Petticoat: Cut two on fold)
(Lining: Cut one on fold)

SKIRT BACK
(follow straight grain, do not cut on fold)
(Main Fabric: Cut two)
(Interlining: Cut two)
(Petticoat: Cut four)
(Lining: Cut two)

Leave open above dot Centre Back only Place to fold of fabric
Cut here for Underskirt Back
Cut here for Underskirt Front
2.5cm (1in) Hem allowance
2.5cm (1in) Hem allowance

Scale 1:6 Each square on the grid represents 2.5cm (1in)   See page 4 for key to pattern markings

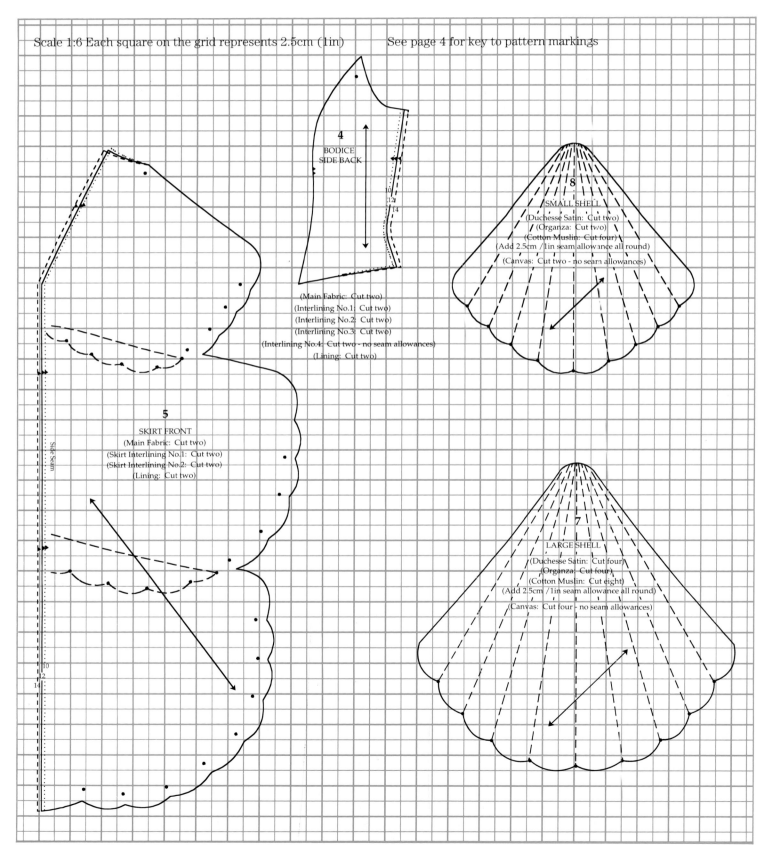

4
BODICE
SIDE BACK

(Main Fabric: Cut two)
(Interlining No.1: Cut two)
(Interlining No.2: Cut two)
(Interlining No.3: Cut two)
(Interlining No.4: Cut two - no seam allowances)
(Lining: Cut two)

5
SKIRT FRONT
(Main Fabric: Cut two)
(Skirt Interlining No.1: Cut two)
(Skirt Interlining No.2: Cut two)
(Lining: Cut two)

Side Seam

10
12
14

8
SMALL SHELL
(Duchesse Satin: Cut two)
(Organza: Cut two)
(Cotton Muslin: Cut four)
(Add 2.5cm /1in seam allowance all round)
(Canvas: Cut two - no seam allowances)

7
LARGE SHELL
(Duchesse Satin: Cut four)
(Organza: Cut four)
(Cotton Muslin: Cut eight)
(Add 2.5cm /1in seam allowance all round)
(Canvas: Cut four - no seam allowances)

Follow the ruching instructions to place a strip around the bustline of a strapless gown. This is a great tip for anyone wishing to achieve a fuller or more shapely bust.

Skirt interlining No 1: 3.60m (4yds) cotton sheeting 140cm (52–54in) wide
Skirt interlining No 2: 3.60m (4yds) stiff net 140cm (52–54in) wide
Lining: 6.20m (6³/₄yds) Poult lining 90cm (35–36in) wide

─────────── TIP ───────────
Instead of purchasing cotton lawn for the bodice, cut the interlining from the cotton sheeting used in the skirt – there will be sufficient in the yardage given.

CHIFFON UNDERSKIRT
Main fabric: 4.50m (5yds) chiffon 115cm (44–45in) wide
Interlining: 4.50m (5yds) Bremsilk lining 140cm (52–54in) wide
Petticoat: 9m (10yds) dress net 140cm (52–54in) wide
Lining: 4.50m (5yds) organza 109cm (43in) wide
Yoke interlining: 90cm (1yd) Duck linen 60cm (24in) wide
(You will only need a total of 1m/1yd to interline the yoke and the panier.)

PANIER
Lining: 90cm (1yd) Poult lining 90cm (35–36in) wide
Interlining: 1.20m (1¹/₃yds) Duck linen 60cm (24in) wide
2m (2¹/₄yds) boning

SHELLS
6m (6¹/₂yds) chiffon 115cm (44–45in) wide
Duchesse satin (you will have sufficient in the yardage purchased for the main dress)
2.70m (3yds) cotton muslin 90cm (35–36in) wide
1.35m (1¹/₂yds) organza 108cm (43in) wide
1.35m (1¹/₂yds) firm collar and cuff canvas 93cm (37in) wide
1m (1¹/₈yd) 56gm (2oz) wadding

NOTIONS
1.40m (1¹/₂yds) satin bias tape 2cm (³/₄in) wide
3.0m (3¹/₄yds) boning
50cm (20in) zip

2 hooks and bars
4 press studs/snap fasteners

─────────── TIP ───────────
Make a much simpler version of this ballgown by eliminating the ruching on the bodice and the ruched shells.

PATTERN PIECES
Bodice: 1 Centre Front, 2 Side Front, 3 Centre Back, 4 Side Back
Skirt: 5 Front, 6 Back, 7 Large Shell, 8 Small Shell, 9 Panier Front, 10 Panier Back
Underskirt: 1 Front & Back Skirt, 2 Side Front and Back, 3 Yoke Centre Front, 4 Yoke Side Front, 5 Yoke Centre Back, 6 Yoke Side Back

─────────── TIP ───────────
The chiffon underskirt is a separate skirt, and not attached to the main gown. You could use the pattern pieces to make a simple evening skirt.

METHODS AND TECHNIQUES
BONED BODICE
ZIP PLACEMENT
RUCHING
MAKING A PANIER
SHELL MAKING
COVERED PRESS STUDS
COVERED HOOK AND BAR
HONG KONG FINISH
FRENCH SEAMS
HAND ROLLED HEM
BABY MACHINED HEM
MACHINE ROLLED HEM
ROULEAUX LOOPS
BUILT-IN WAISTBAND

THE FABRICS
Skirt Interlining No 1 I chose the sheeting for my first interlining layer mainly because I needed a very firm, medium weight cotton. Silk is very static, whereas cotton is dry with an almost hairy finish. Silk will cling to the cotton, keeping the two working well

RIGHT: Once you have completed all the ruching on this stunning gown, you will want to use the technique everywhere. A contrasting fabric ruched to the pocket flaps and cuffs of a jacket can be very effective.

together. The cotton will add a firmness to the fabric and density of colour; essential when using delicate coloured fabrics such as the pale pink satin.

This particular weight of cotton has a depth to it which will add a richness to the silk and more importantly, sheeting has greater width than a dressmaker's cotton lawn, allowing me to cut the very wide skirt patterns in one piece. It is usually acceptable to have joins in interlinings but not in this instance where the light colour and satin finish would allow the joins to show through.

Interlining No 2 Despite the other two layers (main fabric and cotton sheeting), we still lack body. Stiff net, as the name suggests, is a lot stiffer than dress net and will give the body, shape and overall sculptured look we require.

Lining The taffeta finish of poult lining will give body and that delightful rustle when the garment is worn, which always gives a sense of occasion.

CHIFFON UNDERSKIRT

Interlining: Bremsilk lining has been used immediately below the chiffon to add density and to prevent static between the chiffon and the net petticoat.

Petticoat The dress net is light and frothy. I have allowed for two layers to give extra fullness. Gather and stitch the two layers separately to give more bounce.

Lining Organza is a lighter than usual lining but it has body and bounce, and is soft enough to be worn comfortably against the body.

Yoke Interlining Duck linen will give firmness to the yoke. Steam before use for shrinkage.

SHELLS

Cotton muslin will soften the main fabrics and provide a base for attaching the canvas.

Organza provides a firm base for the top of the shell.

Canvas maintains the shape of the shell.

Wadding gives a quilted finish.

METHOD

THE BODICE

1. Take pattern pieces 1, 2, 3, and 4. Cut one set in each of the following fabrics: main fabric, interlining 1, 2, 3, 4 (which has no seam allowances) and lining.

2. Following the Basic Boned Bodice instructions on page 108 complete:
• One Front bodice with boning
• Back bodice with boning.
(Do not insert zip or join side seams at this stage.)

3. We now need to follow the Basic Ruched Bodice instructions (page 116) but with a slight difference. I have chosen to ruche chiffon which is very fine. To achieve the desired effect, it will require double the fabric. I shall therefore use one bias square of chiffon to ruche the bottom half of the bodice and a second bias square to ruche the top half. The two squares will overlap slightly so that any join will be lost in the ruching effect.

Take the boned Front bodice and mark the exact middle with a pin, following the Basic Ruching Technique.

4. Now mark the middle point on the bias chiffon square. Then mark points X and Y on the bias square (see *fig. 5*, page 117).

5. Run one row of gathering thread either side of the centre foldline from point X to point Y.

With bodice Front right side up, place

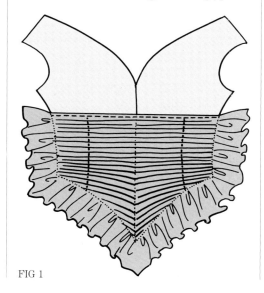

FIG 1

the bias square on the lower half of the bodice, matching both lower points. Match the highest point of the square with the middle point of the bodice, since we are using two bias squares.

6. Pull the gathering threads together, then, with tiny prickstitches, catch the chiffon to the satin across the centre line (*fig. 1*). Trim away excess chiffon above the centre line and prickstitch raw edges in place along the waistline.

7. Now follow the basic instructions for ruching.

8. Repeat the same process for the top half of the bodice. Where the chiffon squares overlap, cut away any excess chiffon, fold in the bottom raw edge of the chiffon and place it over the raw edge already in place at the waistline.

9. Follow the same instructions for ruching the Back bodice which are detailed on page 118.

10. Insert the zip following instructions on page 121.

11. Join the Back and Front bodices at the sides and shoulder seams. Clip and open the seams. Note, the side seams will not be boned.

12. Matching notches and using a 13mm (^{5}/sin) seam allowance, machine all the lining sections together. Following the instructions on page 110, attach the lining to the top edge of the bodice.

13. *Armholes* Clip the armholes all around, up to 3mm (^{1}/sin) away from the canvas. Using a double thread and needle, firmly stitch the seam allowances inwards to the canvas.

14. Bring the lining down, clip the armhole edge and turn in the raw edges. Hand stitch in place using a slipstitch rather than an overstitch.

SKIRT

1. Cut out skirt pattern pieces 5 and 6 in the following fabrics: main fabric, interlining no 1, interlining no 2 and lining.

2. Take the Front and Back skirt pieces in the main fabric and cotton sheeting. Press each piece together (silk to cotton). Now add the net sections. Smooth all three layers so that they are

LEFT: Fine fabrics can be used for a full gathered skirt without adding too much volume to the outline.

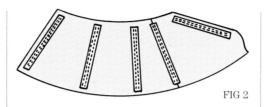

FIG 2

absolutely flat together. Place a few pins in the seam allowance and tack through all layers so that they become one. I recommend the use of a Straw needle and Kinkame silk thread. Tack just 13mm (¹/₂in) from the edge, not directly on the stitching line, so as not to interfere with the machine stitching later.

3. Repeat for all the skirt panels until you have two fully interlined Front and Back skirts.

4. Machine stitch the side seams of the interlined pieces together.

5. Machine the Centre Back seam up to the • marking the bottom of the zip placement. Complete skirt lining to the same stage.

6. Press all seams open using the 3-Point Press (Couture Techniques).

7. Now place the right side of the skirt on the right side of the lining, matching Centre Back, side seams and shell-shaped edges. Pin together.

8. Using the template for each shell piece and a light pencil line, mark the stitching line 15mm (⁵/₈in) from the raw edge. This will give accurate curves and ensure both sides are symmetrical. Now machine, joining the lining to the skirt around all edges, leaving waist seam open. Trim the seam allowance to 10mm (³/₈in); there is no need to layer the seam. Clip into the point of each shell curve.

Turn to the right side, press gently all around the outer edge, ensuring that the lining is pressed slightly to the back rather than visible from the front edge.

PANIER

9. Cut out four of each pattern piece in lining.

Cut two of each pattern piece in linen.

10. Take one pair of Backs in lining and interline with the linen pieces. Repeat for one pair of Fronts. Join at the side seams and press seams open.

11. Cut five pieces of boning which should be positioned evenly across each panel (*fig.2*). The boning should be cut without any seam allowances at the top or bottom.

12. Position by placing one length of

boning over the open seam. Next place one at each end of the panel but do not extend into the seam allowance area. Now place the other two lengths of boning equally between the three already in position. A last piece of boning should now be placed around the bottom edge bending it to the curve as you go.

Machine in place, stitching along the outer edges of the boning lengthwise, ensuring the seam area is left free. These are your top panels.

13. Now machine the side seams of the remaining lining pieces. Press open.

14. Place right side of linings to right sides of top paniers. Machine the front, lower edge and back together, leaving the top edge open. Trim the seam allowance and cut away the corners. Turn to the right side and press lightly.

15. *Attaching the Skirt to the Bodice*
Open flat the Centre Back seam allowance for the zip. With right sides together pin the main skirt to the bodice, matching Centre Back, side seams and fronts. Machine the top skirt in place only. Leave the lining hanging free.

16. With the waistline seam facing upwards to the bodice, place the remainder of the zip in the skirt following the technique employed for the bodice section (page 121).

17. *Attaching the Panier to the Skirt*
Take each side of the panier and drop them inside the skirt, between the main fabric and the lining. The boned and interlined side should be resting against the main fabric.

18. Matching up side seams, fronts and back, machine to the waist seam allowance. Now bring the lining of the main skirt up to the waist and machine in place.

19. Pin around the zip and slipstitch.

20. You will now need a Straw needle

and double thread. I recommend pure silk Gütermann thread for strength. Clip the seam allowance but do not layer. Securely and tightly, stitch all seam allowances of the main skirt, panier, bodice and lining to the muslin of the bodice. Finding the true edge of the canvas at waist level will give a perfect line and a defined point at the bottom of the bodice. Trim any excess bulk around the zip at waist level.

21. Bring down the lining of the bodice, turning in the seam allowance. Pin in place around the zip and waistline; slipstitch. Note, you will be securing the lining to the already secured seam allowance. Continue, stitching the lining of skirt around the zip.

22. Now prickstitch around the hemline and front edge of the skirt to prevent the lining from rolling round to the front. Use Kinkame thread and a Straw needle as this is rather a long job (the fewer knots in the thread, the better). Roll the satin back slightly to the lining, prickstitch through the lining to the interlining about 10–13mm (³/₈–¹/₂in) from the edge, avoiding the seam allowance. Do not go through to the main fabric.

You are now ready for the shells!

RUCHED SHELLS

The following technique will be used for each shell, four large, two small.

1. Cut out the shell template in canvas without any seam allowances.

2. Cut out the template in each of the following fabrics, adding a 2.5cm (1in) seam allowance all the way round, except on canvas: 1 × main fabric, 1 × organza, 2 × muslin and 1 × canvas.

3. Interline the main fabric with one layer of muslin by tacking the two together.

4. Ease the interlined fabric onto the organza. Make stitching guide lines by tacking or pinning. Each line should run from the point of every curve to the centre bottom, to a point just below the curved base (*fig.3*). Now machine along all these lines, from top to bottom and around the outer edge.

5. You should now have three layers machined together (organza, main

RIGHT: Made in white or ivory, this would become a very romantic wedding dress.

FIG 3

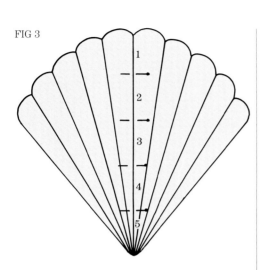

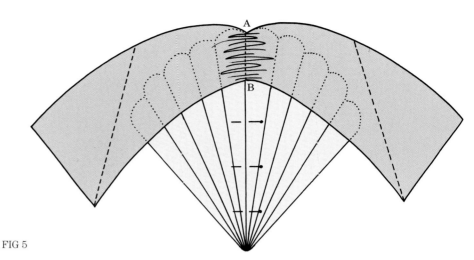

FIG 5

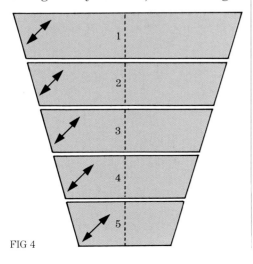

FIG 4

fabric and muslin), the main fabric being slightly fuller than the organza.

6. Make a tiny cut (about 2.5cm/1in) in the organza in each section and fill with the wadding, pushing through a little at a time. I used a screw driver to ensure the wadding went right down to the narrow point. You'll find that the wadding will wrap around the tool, making it quite easy to insert.

7. Take the canvas (minus seam allowances) and place on top of the second layer of muslin and machine 3mm (¹/₈in) inside the canvas edge. The two layers have now become one. Press flat.

8. Stretch the quilted shell over the canvas section making sure that it is the muslin which is visible from the back view. Now machine again over all the shell lines and outer edge, running through all layers. Note, the outer edge

machine line will not include a canvas layer because the canvas has no seam allowance. You are now ready to start ruching the chiffon onto the shell.

RUCHING CHIFFON ONTO SHELL

There are six shells in all; four large and two small.

1. Take five lengths of bias cut chiffon approximately 30.5–37.5cm (12–15in) in width. (The smaller shells will only require four lengths of chiffon.) The length of each piece must be slightly more than the width of the shell.

2. Measure along the centre stitched line of the shell and split this into five equal sections. Mark with pins (*fig.3*).

3. Take the longest length of chiffon, find the centre and run a gathering thread along this line. Use a Straw needle and Kinkame silk thread (*fig.4*).

4. Starting at the top of the shell (i.e. widest point) and stopping at the first pin, draw up the gathering thread so that the chiffon fits between point A and B (*fig.5*). Now pin in between each and every gather. There should be no more than 3mm (¹/₈in) between each pin. Repeat with each length of chiffon, working your way down the shell. At each joining point turn in the raw edge of the next chiffon layer, overlapping the raw edge of the previous one. The raw edge will be lost into the ruching. When you have completely pinned all five layers onto the central line you can machine, using polyester thread, from top to bottom. Remove the pins now.

5. Repeat the process on the next machined line. Mark the five equi-distant points and stretch each layer of chiffon over to these points. Gather up and pin. Carry on this process until the shell is complete, finishing at the sides.

Machine around the outer edge and trim away any excess chiffon.

Note: On the outer edges of the top shell, the longer pieces of chiffon will need to be curved to meet the shape of the shell and trimmed to eliminate excess fabric which will accrue as you work down the curves (*fig.5*).

6. Clip through all layers at each point of the curve. Be extremely careful and cut no closer than 3mm (¹/₈in).

7. Using a Straw needle and double Gütermann silk thread, tightly overstitch the seam allowance, stretching the seam allowance around the canvas and stitch back to the muslin. Take extra care in pulling back around the curves to maintain a good shape. Continue around the shell until all raw edges are taken to the back. Repeat the technique with the five other shells.

―――――――――― TIP ――――――――――

The basic ruching technique can be used in many ways; a fichu collar perhaps, or a ruched halter top.

―――――――――――――――――――――――――

8. *Joining the Shells to the Dress*

With right sides uppermost, place all six shells on the dress, starting at the bottom and overlapping the next as you work your way up the front. Pin in place.

9. Each shell has to be attached by hand stitching. Stitch the underside of the shell to the skirt or shell below, using double silk thread (e.g. Gütermann).

CHIFFON UNDERSKIRT: YOKE

1. Cut two sets of each pattern piece in lining and one set in interlining.

2. Interline one layer of lining with the linen.

3. Join the Fronts, Backs and side seams together.

4. Repeat step 3 with second set of lining which will be used as the lining. Press open all seams.

5. Topstitch all open seams on the interlined section. Put to one side.

6. *Skirt* Cut 1 and 2 in main fabric, interlining, petticoat net and lining. Join all chiffon seams using a French seam. Leave an opening of approximately 15cm (6in) at the Centre Back. Bind with a Hong Kong Finish (Couture Techniques page 115) using bias cut chiffon.

7. *Bremsilk Interlining* Join all seams using French seaming. Leave a 15cm (6in) opening at the Centre Back and Hong Kong Finish again, using the same fabric.

8. *Netted Petticoat* Join all seams by overlapping the net flat and machine stitching one row. Leave a 20.5cm (8in) opening at Centre Back. Repeat for the second layer of net.

9. *Organza Lining* Join all seams with a hairline French seam and Hong Kong Finish the Centre Back opening.

10. *Attaching Skirt Layers to Yoke* Sequence for layers: chiffon skirt, Bremsilk lining, two layers of net, organza.

Take one complete skirt at a time and gather each onto the yoke by matching up side seams, front and backs. Note, the yoke has an overlap for fastening, whereas the skirts will be edge to edge.

——————— TIP ———————

To achieve evenly-spaced gathering always use three rows of gathering thread. Machine approximately 1.5mm (¹/₁₆in) to the left of the seam line, 3mm (¹/₈in) to the right of the seam line and another 3mm (¹/₈in) above that. For fine fabrics, such as chiffon, keep all gathering lines to the right of the seam line, that is, in the seam allowance. Pulling all the threads up together will result in far more even gathers.

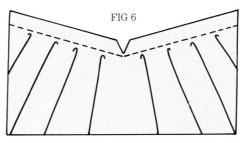

FIG 6

11. Snip into the Centre Front point, up to 15mm (⅝in), before placing the skirt onto the yoke. You can then pivot at the centre and achieve a cleaner point (*fig.6*). Gather both sides of the skirt separately from the Centre Front so as not to break the thread at the snipping point. Pin in place, then machine to the yoke.

12. Repeat the process for all skirt layers. French seams and the organza hairline seam should all be to the inside of the skirt.

——————— TIP ———————

When adding lots of fullness, as in this garment, the gathered seam allowance can become very thick. To make the allowance flatter, machine a second line 6mm (¹/₄in) from the first seam line. Trim up to this second line and machine zigzag over the edge.

13. *Lining the yoke* With right sides together match up the yoke and lining sections. Pin.

14. Machine up the Centre back, along the waist and down the other side. Remember one side has an underlap extension. Trim the seams, cut the corner. Turn to right side and press.

15. All skirt seams should be placed up towards the yoke. Bring the lining down over these, turn under the raw edge and slipstitch in place.

16. Attach four covered press studs (Couture Techniques page 112) down the Centre Back, overlapping left side over the right. Finish with a hook and eye at the waistline.

HEMLINE

1. With all the varying weights of the skirt fabrics and the semi-circular shape of the hem, it is essential that the gown is left to hang before levelling off the hemline. Place it on a hanger and allow it to hang from the top of a door. The fibres need the height so that they can totally relax. Leave to hang for at least a week, longer if possible.

2. When you are ready to hem the skirt place it on a tailor's dummy. Fasten the yoke and ensure that the skirt is sitting correctly. You will need to put the dummy on a high table for ease of working. Have plenty of pins to hand, a tape measure and a hard 30cm (12in) ruler.

Using the tape measure, measure the skirt length you require from the waist down. Add 2.5cm (1in) and mark the spot with a pin in the chiffon only. Now measure up to the pin with the ruler from the table. Inch by inch move the dummy around, placing another pin edge-to-edge with the previous pin. Ensure the chiffon continues to fall in a straight line all the way round. Trim off all excess chiffon.

3. Repeat the same process with the skirt lining, but make this 20mm (¾in) shorter than the chiffon.

4. Next trim the nets so that they are 3.8cm (1½in) shorter than the chiffon. Finally the organza should be trimmed to 5cm (2in) higher than the chiffon.

5. Each layer will now require hemming individually. All the following hem methods can be found in the Couture Techniques section.
Chiffon: Hand rolled hem.
Lining: Baby machined hem.
Net layer: Machine roll the hem using embroidery thread.
Organza layer: Baby machined hem.

THE FINISHING TOUCHES

1. You will need hanging tapes inside the bodice and the chiffon skirt. The nicest way to make these is to make long rouleaux or loops, using scraps of the main fabric for the bodice and lining scraps for the skirt. Follow the Couture Technique on page 116.

2. Cut the rouleaux into two, each 91cm (36in) long. Hand stitch each satin rouleau to the dress by folding the raw

A very beautiful dress for a very special occasion.

edges of one strip together to form a loop. Sit one on top of the other. Place at the waist on the bodice side seam hanging downwards (*fig. 7*). Hand stitch securely through to the seam allowance of the main fabric.

3. Then fold the loop upwards and secure by oversewing approximately 6mm (¹/₄in) up the loop on both sides. Follow the line of the doubled rouleau up the side seam and secure again by hand approximately 7.5cm (3in) from the underarm (*fig.8*). Repeat with second loop.

By distributing the weight of the garment along the length of the loop, you will avoid excessive pulling at any one point.

4. Repeat the process at the waist level of the skirt with the lining loops. The longer length left hanging for the skirt will allow the skirt to sit comfortably

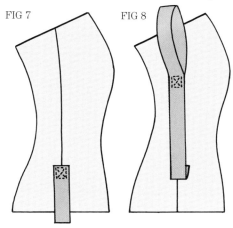

FIG 7   FIG 8

under the main dress on the hanger.

5. *Built-in Waistband* You have probably begun to realize that the gown is becoming a little bit weighty. Most heavy gowns with a boned bodice have a built-in waistband, to avoid any downward pull when worn. To add a built-in waistband to this gown, follow the directions in Couture Techniques (page 121).

6. Now add two hooks and bars; one at the very inside top of the dress and another at waist level, just under the overlap of the zip (on the outside of the garment).

For a more discreet finish, cover the hook and bar (Couture Techniques page 112) before attaching to the gown.

SIMPLY ELEGANT, BEADED GOWN

I have to admit, I'm a wool crepe fan. Wool crepe seems to suit all sorts of design, from the tailored suit to the soft folds in structured dresses. It is certainly a reliable fabric.

While browsing through the wool crepe section on one of my regular fabric store visits I came across the most unusual colour; a hint of peach, tinted with coffee. A very sophisticated shade but not really what I was looking for. Having mentally registered the colour I proceeded to buy my usual four yards of black, or was it navy blue?

On a later visit to the haberdashery department I discovered what had to be one of the bargains of the year. Lengths of silk, two inches wide, which were entirely beaded and embroidered by hand. These exquisite pieces were perfectly stitched in rich cream beads, embroidered with just a hint of gold and at regular intervals a beaded flower in a most subtle shade; a shade I seemed to remember seeing elsewhere.

What a combination! The sophisticated wool crepe with the richly beaded embellishment. Much more interesting than the usual beads and silk dupion. The pairing of beadwork with the drape of crepe brought to mind a simply cut evening gown, wrapped around a tall, slim silhouette, gliding elegantly along a catwalk. Well, perhaps in that scenario it wasn't a gown for me, but nonetheless I set to work on my new creation!

MATERIALS REQUIRED (SIZES 10–14)
Wide fabrics have been used in making this garment; if using a narrow width you may require extra fabric.
Main fabric: 2.90m (3⅛yds) wool crepe 150cm (58–60in) wide
Interlining: 2.90m (3⅛yds) Bremsilk 140cm (54in) wide
Lining: 3.70m (4yds) Habutai silk 90cm (36in) wide
Interfacing: 20cm (¼yd) firm collar and cuff canvas 93cm (37in) wide

NOTIONS
50cm (20in) zip
4.20m (4¾yds) beaded strip 5cm (2in) wide

PATTERN PIECES
1 Centre Front, 2 Side Front, 3 Centre Back, 4 Side Back, 5 Sleeve, 6 Strap.
For interfacing pattern pieces, see notes on main fabric pattern pieces.

THE FABRICS
Main fabric Wool crepe was the only choice for me because the design idea came from the unusual colour of the crepe and the coincidence of finding

beading to match. Other suitable fabrics would include those that drape well, such as a heavy-weight, satin-back crepe or heavy crepe de chine.
Interlining Bremsilk lining was chosen to add density and weight to the fabric without adding bulk. Bremsilk hangs beautifully and will maintain the fluid movement in the dress.
Lining Habutai silk is light and cool to wear. The lining in this garment will be secured all the way round. However, if a design calls for a free-hanging lining, select an alternative as the static of pure silk will cause the lining to ride up.
Interfacing Firm collar and cuff canvas will give a firm, defined edge to the neckline, including the top of the sleeves which, in an off-the-shoulder style, have a tendency to droop. Alternatively use elastic but then you will lose the continuous straight-edged neckline which is very flattering.

METHOD
1. Cut all pieces in main fabric, lining and interlining fabric.
Cut all interfacing pattern pieces without seam allowances.
2. Pick up interlining pieces 1, 2, 3, 4 and 5. Lay the canvas to the wrong side of the interlining 15mm (⅝in) from the edge. Machine 3mm (⅛in) inside the canvas edge and then in rows along the

Use this pattern with a much shorter hemline to create a classic cocktail number, or a summer shift. Add appliqué in place of the beading.

METHODS AND TECHNIQUES
INTERLINING
LINING PLACEMENT
ZIP PLACEMENT
COVERED HOOK AND EYE
COVERED DRESS WEIGHTS
LAYING DOWN A BEADED STRIP

The beaded strip creates a wonderful border to any fabric. Try adding one to an existing jacket, or to a short skirt that needs a little extra length. If the beaded strip has individual motifs, you can cut these out and appliqué them on the body of a garment.

Scale 1:6 Each square on the grid represents 2.5cm (1in)   See page 4 for key to pattern markings

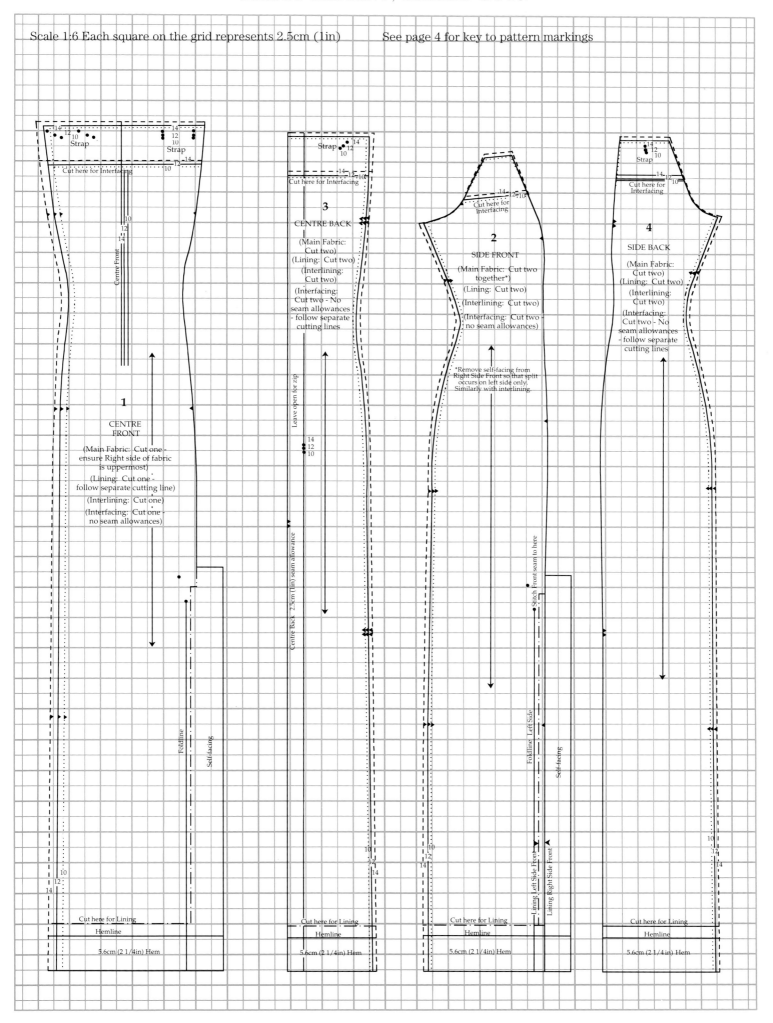

1

CENTRE
FRONT

(Main Fabric: Cut one -
ensure Right side of fabric
is uppermost)

(Lining: Cut one -
follow separate cutting line)

(Interlining: Cut one)

(Interfacing: Cut one -
no seam allowances)

Strap

Centre Front

Cut here for Interfacing

Foldline

Self-facing

Cut here for Lining

Hemline

5.6cm (2 1/4in) Hem

3

CENTRE BACK

(Main Fabric:
Cut two)

(Lining: Cut two)

(Interlining:
Cut two)

(Interfacing:
Cut two - No
seam allowances
- follow separate
cutting lines)

Strap

Cut here for Interfacing

Leave open for zip

Centre Back 2.5cm (1in) seam allowance

Cut here for Lining

Hemline

5.6cm (2 1/4in) Hem

2

SIDE FRONT

(Main Fabric: Cut two
together*)

(Lining: Cut two)

(Interlining: Cut two)

(Interfacing: Cut two -
no seam allowances)

*Remove self-facing from
Right Side Front so that split
occurs on left side only.
Similarly with interlining.

Cut here for
Interfacing

Stitch Front seam to here

Foldline Left Side

Self-facing

Lining Left Side Front

Lining Right Side Front

Cut here for Lining

Hemline

5.6cm (2 1/4in) Hem

4

SIDE BACK

(Main Fabric:
Cut two)

(Lining: Cut two)

(Interlining:
Cut two)

(Interfacing:
Cut two - No
seam allowances
- follow separate
cutting lines)

Strap

Cut here for
Interfacing

Cut here for Lining

Hemline

5.6cm (2 1/4in) Hem

*RIGHT: A simply elegant dress – everybody needs at least
one the wardrobe. With a short hemline, this is a perfect
pattern for that 'little black dress'.*

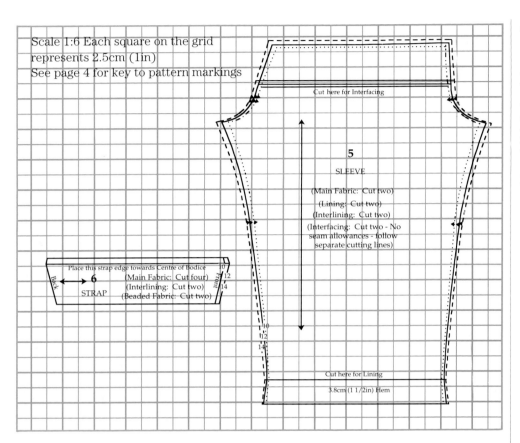

Scale 1:6 Each square on the grid
represents 2.5cm (1in)
See page 4 for key to pattern markings

Cut here for Interfacing

5

SLEEVE

(Main Fabric: Cut two)
(Lining: Cut two)
(Interlining: Cut two)
(Interfacing: Cut two - No
seam allowances - follow
separate cutting lines)

Place this strap edge towards Centre of Bodice

6

STRAP

(Main Fabric: Cut four)
(Interlining: Cut two)
(Beaded Fabric: Cut two)

Back

Front

10
12
14

10
12
14

Cut here for Lining
3.8cm (1 1/2in) Hem

garment), 15mm (⁵⁄₈in) below the neck
edge, along to the underarm seam. Cut
off the strip here, leaving a 15mm (⁵⁄₈in)
seam allowance. Turn in 15mm (⁵⁄₈in) at
the Centre Back. Strip beads from both
seam allowances if necessary to
eliminate bulk (*fig.2*). Repeat the
process for the other side of the Back,
Front and both sleeves (*fig.3*).

FIG 3

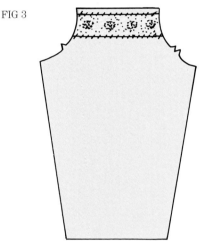

Pay some attention to the pattern (if
any) on your beading, remembering
that some detail will be lost in the seam
allowances. Using a tiny slipstitch,
secure the beaded strip to the main
fabric along both top and bottom edges
and at Centre Back. Secure at the seam
lines.
9. *Straps* Cut four straps in main fabric,
two in interlining and two in beaded
fabric.
10. Mount the interlining to the wrong
side of the two upper straps. Tack the
beaded strip in place on the right side of
the fabric. The seam allowance of the
beading should remain opened out flat
in this case. With right sides together,
pin the lower straps to the upper straps,
making a sandwich of the beading.
Machine along the two long sides of the
rectangle using a zip foot to allow you to
get as close as possible to the
beadwork. Trim only the unlined strap
seam allowance. Turn the straps to the
right side and press from behind.
11. Matching seam allowances, machine
stitch the straps in place at the front
and back neckline.

canvas, approximately 13mm (¹⁄₂in)
apart (*fig.1*). The canvas should be
totally flat to the interlining.
3. Place the interlining to the wrong
side of the main fabric so that the
canvas is still visible. Lightly press each
piece together. Pin and tack the two
layers together and treat as one.
4. Machine Side Fronts to Centre Front
panel, leaving the left side split open

FIG 1

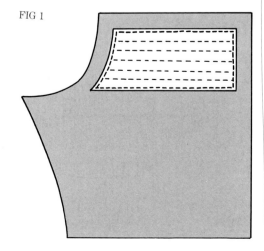

from the notch downwards.
5. Machine the Side Back panels to the
Back panel and machine the Centre
Back seam from the zip notch
downwards.
   Clip seams where necessary and iron
using the 3-Point Press (Couture
Techniques). Press all seams open.
6. Following the zip placement
technique (Couture Techniques), insert
the zip in the Centre Back.
7. Now take the beaded strip and lightly
press the seam allowances to the wrong
side on both edges.
8. Starting at the Centre Back, lay the
strip down (wrong side to right side of
FIG 2

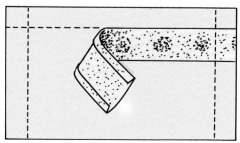

Left: The combination of straps and off-the-shoulder sleeves is both very feminine and easy to wear.

12. Overstitch all top neckline seam allowances on Front, Back and sleeves, down to the interfacing (canvas) layer (*fig.4*).

13. *Sleeves* Machine the side seam of each sleeve. Clip and press open. Turn up the hem and hand stitch to the interlining (*fig.4*).

FIG 4

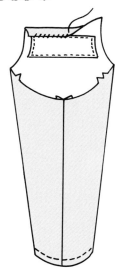

14. Machine the sleeve lining side seams, clip and press open. Turn in 15mm (⁵/₈in) at the top and bottom edges, press (*fig.5*).

FIG 5

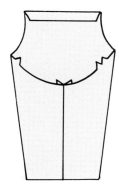

15. With wrong sides together, insert the lining into the sleeve. Bring together the seam allowances at the top of each sleeve (*fig.6*). Slipstitch. Tack around the underarm layers.

16. Bring the sleeve lining down to the top of the cuff hem, overlap the hem by 15mm (⁵/₈in) and slipstitch.

17. Matching side seams, neckline, front and back notches, pin the sleeves

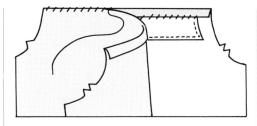

FIG 6

into the main dress and machine in place. Clip up to the stitching line all around the armhole. Oversew the seam allowance down to the interlining of the main dress.

18. *Dress Hemline* To lay down the beaded strip, work as for the neckline but use one continuous strip.

Start by pressing in the seam allowance on the strip and the required hem allowance on the dress. Lay the strip on the foldline of the hem and around the left side opening. You will have to mitre at the top and bottom of the split. Cut away bulk from the corners and secure beading by slipstitching in place (*fig.7*).

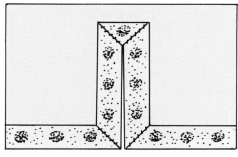

FIG 7

Use a herringbone stitch to secure the hem and side opening back to the interlining.

19. *Lining.* Make up the lining following the instructions for the main dress. Clip all seams and press open. Clip up to the •s at the top of the split (*fig.8*).

Press all lining seam allowances (15mm/⁵/₈in) to the wrong side at the neckline, hemline and side split. The armhole will have to be clipped all the way round in order to turn it back.

20. Drop the lining into the dress, wrong sides together, and pin all folded seams in place along the neckline and

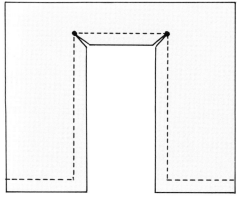

FIG 8

armhole; slipstitch in place.
Bring the lining down, overlap 15mm (⁵/₈in) around the hemline and side split. Slipstitch in place.

FINISHING TOUCHES

21. Hand stitch a covered hook and bar at the top of the zip (refer to Couture Techniques page 112).

──────────── TIP ────────────

The beadwork placed around the hem of this dress is quite weighty and will give a lovely swing to the movement of the dress when worn. If making the dress without the heavy beadwork, you may find that the corners of the split tend to curl outwards. Use covered weights (page 112 Couture Techniques) in both corners, to ensure the split falls in a straight line.

──────────────────────────

Above: A detail of the beaded side split.

3-POINT PRESS

1. Turning fabric to wrong side with seam allowances closed, use the point of the iron *only* to steam press along the line of machine stitches from top to bottom (so as to avoid pressing in puckers).

2. Using only the point of a dry iron, press down the middle of the open seam. It is not necessary to press the seam allowances flat down, as long as they are in an open position.

3. Turn the garment over to the right side. Hover over the seam with the iron, that is, the weight of the iron is not on the garment. The plate is barely touching the surface. With a semi-circular motion hover the iron up the seam and into the fullness of the garment, first to one side and then up, across the other side.

APPLIQUÉ

Featured in the Appliquéd Hat (page 62) and Pink Appliquéd Suit (page 20).

When working LACE APPLIQUÉ it is very important to use a good quality lace. Cotton laces and cotton mixes have a thread running around the outer edge of the pattern. This secures the threads within the pattern and defines the shape. Nylon laces do not have this and therefore fray easily; they are not as pliable for stitching and can look quite bland.

Look very carefully into a piece of lace. What first appears to be a singular, repetitive design can actually be dissected into many shapes and forms, and also re-arranged to create totally different shapes. It is perfect for controlling the finished shape to fit your pattern piece.

Take, for instance, a wedding dress of plain silk dupion. Buy two metres of bordered all-over lace. Cut away the two borders following the intricate design of the pattern. This will give you four metres of interesting border lace for the hem. Working away from the border you will usually find a slightly smaller but similar design. The centre pattern will be smaller still. Cut out many of these, taking care not to cut away the running thread. Try cutting some of the patterns in half or even less; the lace pattern will determine what you can use. Now take the centre front bodice in silk dupion and arrange the lace pieces within this section to any shape you like. The shape tends to dictate the arrangement, such as small leaves trailing off to the points and larger flowers in the centre of the bodice. Quite soon you will see a plain dress turning into a unique creation.

Applying the lace is very simple. Once you are satisfied with the design arrangement, place a pin in the centre of each piece. Thread your machine with a colour to match the lace, not the dupion, as the stitch will be lost into the lace. Set your machine to a small, slightly open zigzag stitch. Start in one corner and zigzag on and off the edge of the design. Your machine foot should have a centre notch. Line this up with the running line of the lace to ensure an even zigzag on both sides. Keep your hand flat on the lace to avoid any puckering and stitch as far as possible without moving your hand. Then stop and adjust, before carrying on. Do not tack before stitching as this will be very restricting. If you have to stretch or ease the lace in any area, you can cut into the piece, following the design, and slightly overlap or open out the shape.

ADDING COLOUR

Take the lace shape and pin it on top of a piece of coloured fabric. Draw a faint line around the shape. Unpin the lace and cut out the coloured shape, ensuring you cut a good 3mm ($^1/_8$in) inside the marker line. Place it under the lace to check that it lies within the shape. Trim where necessary. Now treat the two as one. Pin in place and follow the process above. If you are only adding colour in small areas of the design, use a smaller zigzag stitch which will be lost within the weave of the lace.

For FABRIC APPLIQUÉ you will need an adhesive medium such as Bondaweb/ Wonder Under/Vliesofix to fix the designs to the main garment. You will also need to draw a template of your design.

Cut a square of fabric slightly larger than the template. Take a square of Bondaweb and iron to the wrong side of the fabric. Place the template on the wrong side and trace around it. Cut the shape out and peel off the Bondaweb backing paper. You can now fix the shape onto the garment by pressing in place. Now zigzag around the shape using a thread to match the appliqué fabric in the same way as for lace appliqué but using a closer stitch.

PADDED APPLIQUÉ is the same as above, with the addition of a layer of domette fixed to the first square of appliqué fabric with Bondaweb. The complete sequence of layers will be: appliqué fabric, Bondaweb, domette, Bondaweb, main garment.

Once attached to the main garment, zigzag as above.

THE BASIC BONED BODICE

The following technique can be used for any bodice pattern, including those featured in this book.

For a basic boned bodice there are generally four pattern pieces. This may vary with the garment style.

These are:

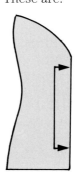

CENTRE FRONT PANEL   FRONT SIDE PANEL

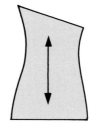
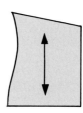

SIDE BACK PANEL   CENTRE BACK PANEL

Cutting Out

Using the four pattern pieces cut one set from each of the following materials:
Note: I suggest you add on to your seam allowance at the Centre Back, making it 2.5cm (1in). This will accommodate the zip. All other seam allowances will be 15mm (⁵/₈in) unless otherwise stated.
A. The main bodice fabric, for example, silk dupion, taffeta, satin.
B. Interlining
1. Use a light to medium weight cotton, matching the exact colour of your main fabric. This is particularly important in bridalwear as any varying shades underneath will affect the colour of your bodice and skirt, although sometimes slight colour differences cannot be avoided.
2. Domette or an additional cotton layer. This is a second layer of interlining which is not always required. It will add density and softness to finer fabrics and will also prevent stitching and boning showing through.
C. Canvas. Use a firm collar and cuff canvas. Unlike the other layers, this must *always* be cut without any seam allowances and therefore without the 2.5cm (1in) Centre Back allowance for the zip.

——————— TIP ———————
It is a good idea to have another set of pattern pieces for the canvas, removing all the seam allowances. Lay these patterns onto the canvas and use a fine sharp pencil to draw around them; then cut all the pieces out.
——————————————————

D. Cotton Muslin. Not too loosely woven, this will be used to anchor down your hand stitching from the inside.
E. Lining. If possible use poult lining, a light taffeta lining with a slight rib, which has body without being too thick. Try to keep to medium weights. Anything too thin will show stitching through and may cause scratchiness from the boning. A lining that is too thick will add unwanted bulk.

——————— TIP ———————
For summer dresses such as a Caribbean holiday or wedding, use cotton lawn as your lining. This will be cool next to the skin.
——————————————————

You should now have five of each pattern piece or six if you have used the extra interlining layer. Put them into groups of backs, fronts etc. to help you organize your work.

Bodice Construction

These bodices are very sturdy and are built from the inside to the outside. So we start first with the canvas (C) and the interlining fabric (B1).
1. Before using the canvas pieces trim 1.5mm (¹/₁₆in) all the way round. This will ensure that the canvas is completely clear of the seam allowance and thus maintain the correct bodice size. At this stage you should check every canvas piece against the adjacent piece to ensure they are of equal length. If not, this will distort the finished edge of the bodice. Check and trim where necessary.

Now take all the canvas pieces and place them on top of the first layer of corresponding interlining pieces (light cotton). Pin them in place using just a few pins as the canvas is very stiff.

Machine stitch together around all edges, 1.5mm (¹/₁₆in) inside the canvas edge. Remember, the canvas has no seam allowances. You must keep the canvas flat to the fabric to avoid creating any air pockets (*fig.1*).

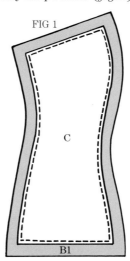

FIG 1

C

B1

Canvas now covered by muslin FIG 2

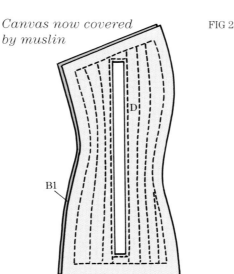

D

B1

Place the cotton muslin (D) on top of the canvas and machine 1.5mm (¹/₁₆in) inside the canvas edge again.

Now machine stitch in vertical lines 13mm (¹/₂in) apart, quilting the canvas completely (*fig.2*).

Machine a length of boning through the centre of each bodice piece, ending about 13mm (¹/₂in) away from the top and bottom edges of the canvas (*fig.2*).

Stitch along all four edges of the boning, not just down the centre. This will stabilize the boning, preventing it from rolling.

——————— TIP ———————
Where a Centre Front bodice is long and pointed (e.g. the Pink Ballgown), take the boning all the way into the point and to the very edge of the canvas. This will give a good point and stops it from wrinkling or curling up.
——————————————————

2. Take these completed pieces and place them on top of the second interlining layer if used (B2), that is, place the lightweight cotton against the domette.

Machine stitch 3mm (¹/₈in) from the outside edge of the canvas. Thus all the interlining pieces have become one.
3. Now place the wrong side of the main fabric on top of the interlining fabric layer (*fig.3*). Pin and machine stitch 6mm (¹/₄in) from the outside edge of the canvas.

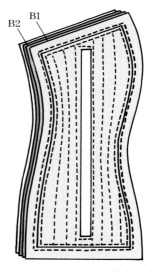

B1
B2

FIG 3

You should now have all four bodice sections constructed to the same stage. The lining fabric is yet to be built in.
4. Join the layered Side Front panels to Centre Front panel. Machine stitch just outside the canvas, clip seams.

——————— TIP ———————
Work with the Side panels uppermost so that the fullness will be on the top, giving you greater control. Stretch the curve into the straighter line.
——————————————————

Machine the Side Back panels to Centre Back panels.

Clip all seams but do not trim any seam allowances.

5. Insert the zip following steps 1–7 in Couture Techniques (page 121).

6. The following boning instructions apply to all bodice seams except the side seams.

Have the bodice section wrong side uppermost and lightly press all seams open with the point of the iron. Working one seam at a time, take the satin bias seam tape and place it centrally along the length of the seam (wrong side down). Attach to the seam allowances *only* by machine stitching along both edges of the tape. Be sure to let the seam open naturally; avoid pulling the tape too tight or feeding it through too loosely (*fig. 4*).

FIG 4 *The casing for the boning*

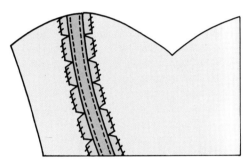

FIG 5

Take a length of boning and push it through the tape slot you have created. The boning should be kept within the canvas edge at the top and bottom of the bodice.

Now hand stitch all the open seams to the muslin. You will need a Straw needle for this. Do not stitch through to the front of the bodice (*fig. 4*).

7. Machine the bodice side seams together just outside the edge of the canvas. Clip and open.

8. Join all the lining pieces together by machine stitching. Clip and press open seam allowances. With right sides together and matching seams, pin in place along the top edge of the bodice. Machine stitch just outside the canvas edge.

Clip seams and into centre point, taking care not to cut the stitching line. Do not trim or layer the seams.

Using a needle and double thread, hand stitch all the layers of the seam allowance at top edge tightly to the muslin, rolling seam line slightly down to the inside so that it cannot be seen from the right side of the bodice (*fig. 5*).

At Centre Back turn the raw edge of the lining inside to create a foldline to meet the zip at either side. Pin in place. Using tiny prickstitches around the top and side edges of the bodice, hand sew

the lining in place, always rolling slightly to the wrong side of the bodice (*fig. 6*). Prickstitch around the zip but still leaving enough free at the bottom (7.5cm/3in) to attach the skirt.

Note: You will be stitching through the lining to the seam allowance only – not through to the main fabric of the garment. You have already secured the seam allowances to the muslin.

Complete the bodice with a hook and bar placed above the zip fastening on the top edge. Cover the hook and bar using the Couture Technique (page 112).

This is as far as you can go with a basic bodice before making the skirt. Completely finish the skirt to your design or pattern instructions, remembering to leave part of the Centre Back seam open for the rest of the zip. Seam allowance should be 2.5cm (1in) wide.

Note: If making a bodice with sleeves, these should be sewn in place before lining.

BONED CUFF
(Pink Appliquéd Suit, page 20)

This technique gives a very dramatic finish to a garment and can be used on the finest silk suit or the most luxurious velvet evening coat. Whatever the construction of the garment you apply it to, the technique for forming the cuff will be the same.

Take the cuff pattern and cut the following: 4 × main fabric, 2 × domette, 2 x cotton lawn, 2 × firm collar and cuff canvas (without seam allowances). You will also need boning 13mm (1/2in) wide cut to the required length.

The canvas forms the finished edge of the cuff, so when machining you will have to ensure that no canvas is sewn in the seam allowance. However, the canvas must be secured to prevent movement. You must therefore first combine the canvas with the cotton lawn to form the required firm foundation with a soft seam allowance.

Work as follows:

1. Take the canvas and place it in the centre of the cotton lawn. Press the two together and pin to secure. Do check that you have two opposites; one left, one right cuff. Now machine 3mm (1/8in) inside the canvas edge, ensuring the two layers are absolutely flat to each other. Then machine quilt the two layers by stitching in parallel lines 13mm (1/2in) apart.

2. Take a length of boning and place on the canvas just inside the back side seam, cutting to shape and ensuring

FIG 6 *Inside the lined bodice*

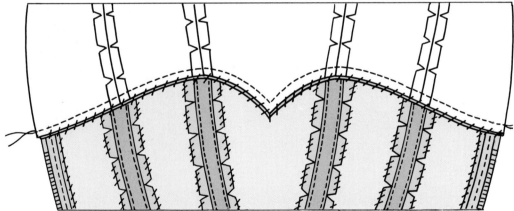

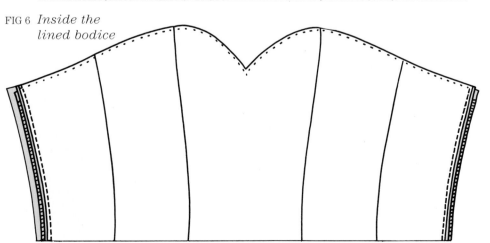

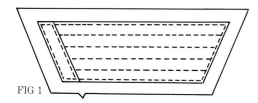

FIG 1

that it does not extend beyond the canvas (*fig.1*). Machine around all four edges of the boning to prevent rolling.

3. Place the flat side of the cotton lawn down to the domette. Machine on the very edge of the canvas. Now place the domette to the wrong side of the main fabric. Note how all the work on the inside is masked by the density and richness of the domette. If the main fabric has depth already, you may wish to omit the domette and place the cotton lawn straight onto the main fabric. Check the effect first.

4. Now machine 6mm (¼in) outside the canvas edge, making all layers one. This will be your Top cuff. Machine the side seams together and repeat for the Under cuff. Press all seams open. Place Top and Under cuffs right sides together and machine around the top edge 3mm (⅛in) outside the canvas edge. Layer the seam.

5. Turn cuff through to right side and machine Top and Under cuff together at the hemline, 6mm (¼in) outside the canvas edge. The cuff is now complete and ready to be joined to the sleeve.

BUTTONHOLES

BACK TO FRONT BUTTONHOLE

This technique can be very useful when:

a. You have several interlayers adding bulk to a garment; machine-worked buttonholes have a tendency to look very thin.

b. You need a large buttonhole to take those extra big buttons. I'm quite partial to the larger buttons and these days there is a wonderful selection for the dressmaker. But large buttonholes can look quite ugly and even distort the hang of a garment.

In both cases I would recommend the following method.

1. Place the jacket right front, right side up, on a flat surface. Using your pattern mark the button positions. Hand stitch them in place, through all layers into the facing. Use a double thread or strong tailoring thread.

2. On the underside of each button place a much smaller one, such as a shirt button. Attach the button with a thread shank, i.e. place a pin or matchstick above the button and sew it on by sewing over the top of the pin. Remove the pin and pull the button up

to the top of the stitches so that you now have a shank of thread (about 3mm/⅛in) between the button and the garment. Wrap the sewing thread tightly around the shank several times and then backstitch through the shank several times to secure. This shank will make it easier to fasten the button.

3. Mark the position of the small buttons on the opposite jacket front and make your small buttonholes to correspond. When fastened the buttonholes will be invisible.

BOUND BUTTONHOLE

This buttonhole is created entirely by hand. Without the worry of putting it all under the machine, you can easily control the finished result.

─────── TIP ───────
Work on the ironing board as you will need to press as you go. Also, make one buttonhole at a time so that the fusible web remains hot while you work.

You will need :
An extra piece of your selected fabric for the bound area.
Narrow piping cord (I recommend 3mm / ⅛in diameter or wider for thicker fabrics.)
Adhesive web (e.g. Bondaweb/Wonder Under/Vliesofix).
Pencil and ruler

1. Take a piece of Bondaweb approximately 7.5cm (3in) square. On the smooth side draw a line the length of your required buttonhole and lines across the top and bottom to indicate depth of buttonhole (*fig.1*).

2. Now draw a line either side of the first line to the diameter of your piping cord, in this case 3mm (⅛in). Trim the Bondaweb leaving approximately 15mm (⅝in) all around the buttonhole. When you are happy with the size of the buttonhole, make as many as you will need for your garment.

3. Cut two pieces of cord to the length of the finished buttonhole, for example,

a buttonhole measuring 3.2cm (1¼in). Cut two strips of fabric to cover the cord 2.5cm (1in) wide and 5cm (2in) long. Tack the fabric around the cord to keep it in place.

4. On the wrong side of the garment fabric, place the Bondaweb rectangle in the required buttonhole position. Fuse to the wrong side, following the manufacturer's instructions. With small scissors cut up through the middle of the buttonhole and into all four corners (*fig.2*).

5. Now peel off the Bondaweb backing paper and fold back all raw edges of the buttonhole to create a perfect rectangle on the right side. The raw edges will all stick in place due to the adhesive left from the web (*fig.3*). A thicker fabric will require firm pressing with the point of the iron.

6. Working from the right side of fabric, place the covered piping cord under the buttonhole, ensuring the cord rests evenly and does not extend beyond the hole (*fig.4*). Press, using a pressing cloth and the complete weight of the iron. Now you must secure it by hand sewing.

FIG 3   FIG 4

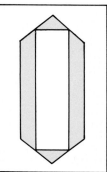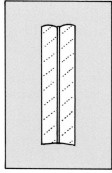

7. Take a Betweens needle and single Kinkame thread. Secure the needle and thread to the back of the buttonhole. Come through to the right side of the garment and starting in one corner, make a small stitch through the main fabric then slipstitch over into the groove of the piping cord. Go under and along 3mm (⅛in), come up into the main fabric and immediately back down into the groove of the cord. Pull the stitches tight so that they sink right into the fabric and do not sit on the top. Continue all the way around the buttonhole.

THE BACK OF THE BUTTONHOLE

In most cases the back is covered by a facing. In rare cases it may be covered by the lining, e.g. in a man's waistcoat. Whichever, the buttonhole back will always be the last item to be completed

FIG 1   FIG 2

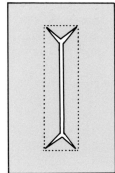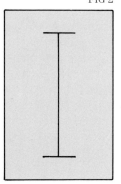

on any garment. You will then know that your facing or lining is laying perfectly flat to the main garment. Always check for rippling.

8. Place a pin at either end of the buttonhole at the middle point, pushing from the front through to the back and into the facing. Turn to the back so that you are now looking at the facing. With small scissors make a slit through the middle and cut to either side of the pins (*fig.5*). Take out the pins, tuck under the raw edges of the facing or lining and oversew in place.

FIG 5

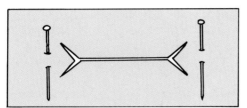

HAND FINISHED BUTTONHOLES
These can often be neater than those made by machine and will add an attractive finish to a garment.

1. First mark the buttonhole position and size using a small, open zigzag machine stitch. This will provide an even guideline for the buttonhole width and a firm foundation to work on. Do not finish off or bar tack at either end.

2. Cut through the middle of the buttonhole using small scissors. Start half-way up one side of the buttonhole working buttonhole stitch all the way round to the starting point. I recommend Gütermann's silk thread and a Betweens needle.

3. Instead of a bar tack at each end, spread the buttonhole stitch around the curves to give a neat arch (*fig.1*). A bar tack can be worked on the inside of the buttonhole at each end.

FIG 1

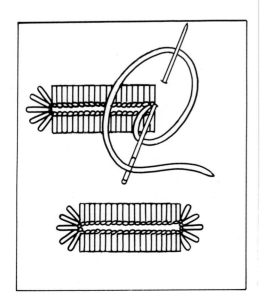

COVERED DRESS WEIGHTS
1. Take a round lead dress or curtain weight and cut a circle of lining fabric approximately 13mm (¹/₂in) larger than the weight.

2. Turn in 3mm (¹/₈in). With a needle and thread sew a row of running stitches around the edge. Draw up the stitches, encasing the weight. Secure the thread at the back.

3. Slot the covered weight inside the dress hem (particularly at the corners in the case of the Beaded Gown, page 100). To keep the weight in position, hand stitch the edge of the covered weight to the hem on the inside of the dress. Complete the hem as usual.

COVERED HOOKS, EYES AND BARS
For a discreet fastening.

Using a Betweens needle and Gütermann silk thread, work close buttonhole stitch around the complete bar, hook or eye. It is easier to cover the fastener before attaching to the garment.

COVERED PRESS STUDS/SNAPS
Use this technique to cover metal press studs. When closed, they will be barely visible. The technique is very similar to covering buttons.

1. Cut a circle of self fabric, slightly bigger than both pieces of the press stud. Snip a very tiny hole in the middle of the circle, just enough to separate the threads. Push the nipple of the stud through the hole. Run a gathering thread around the outer edge of the circle and draw it up. Oversew the back of the stud to flatten the raw edges.

2. Now stitch the covered press stud in position on the garment by catching the very edge of the stud to the fabric. Continue all the way round, without sewing through the stud holes.

3. Repeat the technique for the other side but do not make a hole in the centre. The stud will close easily by pushing the fabric into the middle.

DARTS
The following technique applies to making all darts. You will notice that I interline all my garments and that the darts are prepared when the pattern pieces have been interlined. Darts are not prepared on each separate layer.

1. Lay the corresponding pattern piece on top of each interlined section. Use pins to mark each • symbol denoting the line of stitching for the dart. Where you have cut more than one of a pattern piece, the two can be laid on top of each other, right sides facing. In this case,

push another pin through from the underside so that the dart position is marked by pins on both pieces. Separate the two pieces.

2. Match up the pin markings, drawing the fabric together with right sides facing. Re-pin in the direction you will follow when machine stitching. You will start at the widest point, finishing at the tip (*fig.1*).

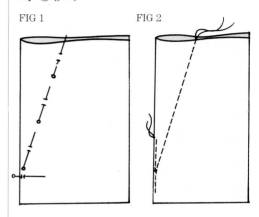

FIG 1   FIG 2

3. Machine stitch down to the final pin denoting dart point and then continue beyond, making approximately four stitches on the very edge of the fold and then reversing off (*fig.2*).

These last four stitches will make the dart point flat. It is vital that they sit on the very edge to prevent them showing through on the front.

DEEP POINTED COLLARS AND REVERS
(Pink Appliquéd Suit, page 20)
The neckline can be one of the most flattering aspects of any creation. It's like choosing a picture frame; you are the picture, the collar the frame.

The Pink Suit has quite a dramatic structure. Consistency of style is maintained with the deep pointed collars and revers. The Top collar has been created in almost the same way as the Boned Cuff, but the making up of Top to Under collar is slightly different, due to the very long points. Turning any point through can be difficult, but these are a nightmare! The technique used here can be used for any awkward point, for example, waistcoats, a Dior Cuff, pocket flaps and revers.

For the Pink Suit you will need the collar and revers pattern pieces. Cut the following:
Collar: 2 × main fabric*, 1 × cotton, 1 × firm collar and cuff canvas (no seam allowance), 1 × domette.
*The Under collar could be cut in a lining fabric if, for example, the main fabric is very thick.
Revers: 4 × main fabric, 2 × cotton, 2 × firm collar and cuff canvas (no seam

allowance), 2 × domette.

If using a Double Edge Binding, remember that the top layers of the collar and revers will already be bound.
1. Follow the instruction for the boned cuff from cutting out stage to attaching the main fabric, omitting the use of boning. You should now have completed a Top collar and two Top revers.
2. Take the Top collar and overstitch by hand the seam allowance down to the canvas. Use a Straw needle and double Gütermann silk thread, pulling the seam allowance firmly so that the canvas clearly defines the edge. Mitre the corners strongly, using the canvas to work around (*fig.1*). Do this by firmly folding the seam allowance around the canvas so that you form a crease. Open up the allowance to trim away any bulk. The crease line will show you what can be cut away but take care you do not cut away too much!

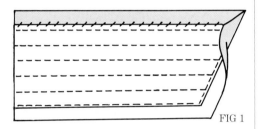

FIG 1

Ladder stitch up the mitre to keep the point secure. If a point is very long and thin you may have to make two folds in the mitre corner.
3. Place the collar wrong side uppermost, laying the Under collar on top, wrong sides together. Turn under the seam allowance of the Under collar, making sure it rests slightly towards the underside. Match Centre Back and outer edges by mitring points and pin in place (*fig.2*).

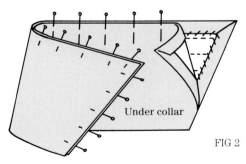

Under collar

FIG 2

4. Slipstitch all round the outer edges with tiny stitches, leaving the neck edge open. Repeat the technique for the revers. Now continue with the neckline construction.

DOUBLE-EDGE BINDING
(Pink Appliquéd Suit, page 20)
Single edge binding is a favourite couture technique. Used by the top

designers, the finished look gives the false impression of hand-bound edges. The binding is actually a flat pattern piece, stitched to the collar or elsewhere, before construction. Double binding is the same process repeated, using two different widths of contrasting fabrics. The technique can be used on any design but you will need to cut a pattern for the edging first. The binding pattern pieces are given for the Pink Suit.

Making a Binding Pattern
If you were to make your own pattern, you would use the main garment pattern as a starting point, for example, the front edge of a jacket.
1. From the seam allowance on the main pattern draw your required width of binding, (e.g. 2.5cm/1in). Now add a 15mm ($^5/_8$in) seam allowance all around, still following the line of the main pattern (*fig.1*). Trace this off, keeping the grain. This is your single edge binding pattern (*fig.2*). For a double edge, repeat the process, making the binding a different width e.g. 20mm ($^3/_4$in).

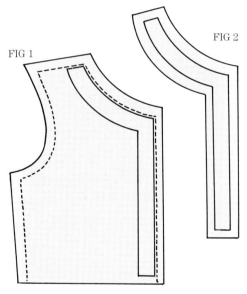

FIG 1

FIG 2

Applying the Binding
I will use the Top collar from the Pink Suit to demonstrate construction.
2. Cut one wide binding strip in grey grosgrain. Cut one narrow binding strip in pink grosgrain.
3. Take the narrow strip and clip up to the large dots in the corners of the inside seam allowance. Turn the seam allowance to the wrong side and press (*fig.3*).
4. Lay this on top of the wide strip, having the wrong side of the narrow strip facing the right side of the wide strip. Match up the outer edges (*fig.4*).
5. Fold down the top edge of the

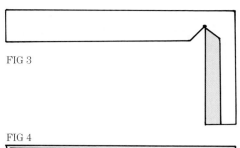

FIG 3

FIG 4

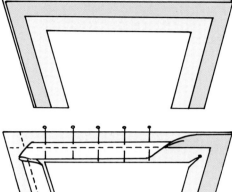

FIG 5 *Machine across the corners*

narrow width to reveal the pressed seam allowance. Pin on the seam line (*fig.5*).
6. Machine seam allowance straight across the long top edge first, making sure you secure the corners. Remove pins and press back up lightly.

Fold back at the sides to reveal pressed seam allowance, pin and machine. Remove pins and press back.
7. Tack along the three outer edges, joining the two bindings together.
8. Now clip up to the notches in the corner of the inside of the wide strip. Press seam allowance back to the wrong side. Lay the binding on top of the Top collar, wrong side of binding facing right side of collar.
9. Lift the top edge back to reveal the seam allowance. Pin and machine straight across. Repeat for both sides ensuring you secure both corners.
10. Remove pins and lightly press back up. Tack the outer edge. The Top collar is now complete and you can continue with the construction (*fig.6*). The Under collar does not require binding.

FIG 6 *Top collar now complete*

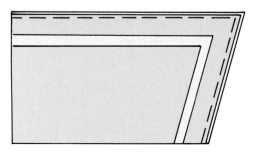

FRENCH SEAM

This neat seam should not be too wide or bulky. Use on very fine fabrics to encase raw edges.

1. Start by stitching your seam with wrong sides together and taking only 10mm (³/₈in) seam allowance. Sew a second seam immediately next to this, towards the raw edge. Now trim as close as possible to the second stitching line (*fig.1*). This second row will prevent threads coming through to the right side. Press twice.

2. Bringing fabric right sides together, make a sharp edge of the stitching line. Now enclose the two rows of stitching by machining a line 3–4.5mm (¹/₈–³/₁₆in) from the seam edge (*fig.2*). The finished width of the seam will be a maximum 4.5mm (³/₁₆in). Press lightly.

FIG 1   FIG 2

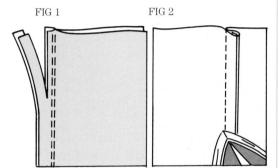

HAIRLINE FRENCH SEAM

This seam is very tiny but quite strong.

Join the seams together as above, but taking a 13mm (¹/₂in) seam allowance. Stitch the second row no more than 1.5mm (¹/₁₆in) away. Trim and press flat. Turn fabric so right sides are facing and press again. Encase the two rows of stitching and raw edges with a small, slightly open zigzag stitch. Using the machine foot as a guide, sew on and off the edge. The finished seam allowance will only be the width of the zigzag stitch.

HEM TECHNIQUES

BABY MACHINED HEM

For a 6mm (¹/₄in) hem: Turn in the raw edge 3mm (¹/₈in) and machine. Turn in another 3mm (¹/₈in) and machine again.

CURVED HEM

It is very difficult to obtain a neat finish on curved hems, because you are turning a longer line into a shorter line. This can cause puckers and a generally uneven finish. I use a binding to eliminate the problems. There are two techniques, one for light fabrics, the other for heavier weights. In both cases the first step is to cut the original hem allowance back to 15mm (⁵/₈in).

a. Light fabrics: e.g. silk crepe de chine and silk satin. Obvious examples are the full circular skirt or shirt tails.

1. Cut a bias strip of the required hem circumference, making bias joins where necessary. The strip should be twice the required width plus 3.2cm (1¹/₄in). For example, if a hem is to be 20mm (³/₄in), the strip will be 7cm (2³/₄in) wide.

2. Fold the strip in half lengthways, wrong sides together and press. Pin the double raw edge to the garment edge, right sides together and easing around the curve.

3. Now machine all the way round, taking a seam allowance of 15mm (⁵/₈in) from the raw edges (*fig.1*). Trim this to 6mm (¹/₄in). Press the seam flat towards the strip.

FIG 1

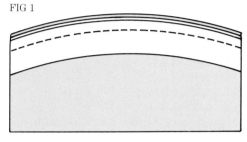

4. Now press the strip and seam up to the garment on the inside, using the seam line to give a sharp, curved hemline. Slipstitch the folded edge to the main fabric. Press lightly from the front.

b. Heavier weight fabrics: e.g. light and medium weight wool, linen etc.

Follow the above technique but use only a single layer of fabric, machining in 15mm (⁵/₈in) at the bottom of the hem and blindstitching the upper edge to the main fabric. Neaten this upper edge before blindstitching.

FALSE HEM

I would use this hem mainly for ballgowns, bridalwear and special occasion wear. In actual fact it is a facing rather than a hem, applied for the following reasons.

1. The gown may have a circular or unusual hemline, for example, shorter at the front and drifting into a long train at the back.

2. Quite often net is used as an interlining in the main skirt. If this gets caught it will rip and drop below the hemline. Where a false hem has been used, it may come away but will not drop below the firmer hemline.

3. The stitching line will add weight and a definite edge for the skirt to sit properly.

4. If you are adding a second or even third interlining in the hemline (e.g. domette for a rich, padded finish or organza for a roll effect), the seamline can be used to secure any of these layers in place.

Cutting false hems

Cut your facing by using the bottom of the appropriate pattern piece. Cut off the hem allowance on the garment leaving a 15mm (⁵/₈in) seam allowance. On the tissue, ignore the hemline and mark your required hemline plus 15mm (⁵/₈in). Cut away the rest.

Following the shape of this line, draw another line approximately 10cm (4in) inside the hemline, following the same grain as the main garment. This 10cm (4in) strip will be your false hem pattern piece. Cut out the facing or false hem in main fabric only.

In my experience, if you join all the pieces together before attaching to the skirt you will never achieve the same measurement as the hem edge. So place each section individually as follows.

1. Start at the front (*Section A fig.1*). Place the facing to the skirt at hemline, right sides together. Turn back the seam allowance to wrong side at each end of facing to match the skirt seamlines. Pin facing to the skirt.

2. Now position the next facing section (*Section B fig.1*), lapping the flat seam allowance over the adjacent turned-back seam allowance. Turn in the seam allowance at the other end.

FIG 1

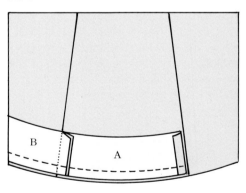

3. Continue in the same manner so that each section will have a turned-back edge and a flat, overlapping edge except section A. Thus you can adjust as you go round to ensure an exact measurement fit to all seam lines. Pin all the way round and machine 15mm (⁵/₈in) in from the raw edges.

4. Trim the allowance down to 10mm (³/₈in), clipping where necessary. Press the facing seam flat and then press upwards to the wrong side of the main fabric. The seamline should be kept slightly to the wrong side of the garment. Turn in the raw hem edge 15mm (⁵/₈in) and pin to the net or interlining layer. Prickstitch facing to net or interlining only, along hem edge and down seams for a secure finish.

ADDING HORSEHAIR BRAID

This braid is used to add stiffness to the hemline of the lining, usually found in bridal and special occasion wear.

1. Place the false hem or facing to the lining hemline as above. After machining press the seam flat down towards the false hem (*fig.1*). Now lay the braid on top of the seam allowance up to the stitching line. Lay the braid around the entire hem, overlapping where the braid meets.

FIG 1

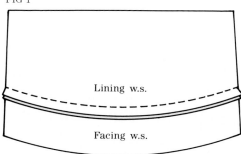

Lining w.s.

Facing w.s.

2. Machine stitch along the edge of the braid, just below the stitching line (*fig.2*), through all the allowance layers but not through the facing. Turn in the outer edge seam allowance of the facing and press.

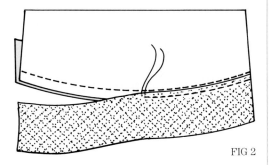

FIG 2

3. Now turn this up to the inside of the garment, encasing the braid. Machine in place without stitching through the braid.

HAND ROLLED HEM

This technique is used where a very narrow hem is required, for example, on fine fabrics such as chiffon. First, you must remember to add 13mm (½in) to the required hem length before cutting out the piece.

Machine stitch 13mm (½in) from the raw hem edge. Trim up to the stitching line. Holding needle and thread in your right hand, use your left hand to roll the fabric around the machine stitching, using your thumb and forefinger. The

machine stitching will give the fabric something stable to roll around. Roll tightly to the wrong side, so that the fabric wraps approximately twice around the stitching line. Slipstitch the roll to the main fabric. I recommend a fine Betweens needle and Kinkame thread for chiffon fabric.

MACHINE ROLLED HEM

A pretty edging and one recommended for net to eliminate a coarse edge finish. You will need a roll hemming foot on your machine, polyester thread and six-strand DMC embroidery thread.

Thread the machine with a good quality polyester thread. Set the machine to a small, slightly open zigzag stitch.

Push the edge of the net through the roll hemming foot so that it wraps around itself with the zigzag stitch, at the same time feeding through the embroidery thread which will be encased by the zigzag stitch. At the end you will need to overlap the embroidery threads, laying one on top of the other.

HONG KONG FINISH

Use on exposed seams and fine fabrics for a professional finish.

Cut a bias strip of fabric 3.8cm (1½in) wide and the required length. Fold in half lengthwise and press. Place the double raw edge down to the raw edge to be bound (right sides together). Machine 6mm (¼in) from the edge. Sew a second row and trim the raw edges.

Bring the double bias strip over the raw edge and press. Fold the strip to the wrong side, encasing the raw edge and press. Slipstitch the fold edge to the first row of machining. Press.

JACKET LINING PLACEMENT

Applying jacket linings should be one of the easiest things to do. The first thing to remember is to transfer any alterations to the main fabric jacket pattern to your lining pattern.

You will notice that the lining pieces are cut longer and wider; this is for seating and ease. As long as you are consistent with alterations and seam allowances, it will be impossible for the lining to be too long or too short.

Another frequent problem or frustration occurs when the lining meets the facing at the hemline. Follow these simple instructions to avoid such problems.

1. Machine all darts and panels together to form Front and Back linings. Clip and press seams open. Press darts towards the centre.

2. Machine side seams and shoulder seams. Clip and press open. Machine sleeve seams, clip and press. Set in the sleeves, clip and press.

3. Press in a 15mm (⅝in) seam allowance on all the outer edges, clipping where necessary. Matching up Centre Back, side seams and Fronts, place the lining to the top of the jacket hemline, resting the 15mm (⅝in) seam allowances of facings and lining together. A pleat will form at the lower edge which will fall towards the bottom of the jacket, allowing ease when worn (*fig.1*). Pin in place then slipstitch to secure.

By laying the hem first instead of last you should find it easier to fit the lining.

FIG 1 *Slipstitch to the hemline*

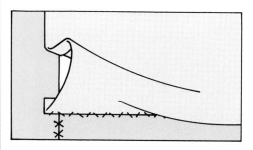

4. Now take the lining to meet the facing at the neck edge, overlapping facing edge by 15mm (⅝in), and matching up Centre Backs and shoulder seams. Pin in place.

5. Bring the lining down the front facings, matching notches and still overlapping 15mm (⅝in). Continue to your starting point at the hemline where the natural pleat will form. Repeat for other jacket front. Pin in place and slipstitch all the way round to secure completely, using Kinkame thread and a Betweens needle. Remove all pins.

6. Bring the lining down into the sleeves, matching up seams. Pin the lining by overlapping 15mm (⅝in) to the hem top, slipstitch to secure.

7. Look inside the jacket to match up shoulder seams at the armhole edge. Secure the lining with a bar tack through to the shoulder pad or the seam of the jacket. Press lightly.

LAYERING SEAMS

Layer or trim seam allowances after stitching to eliminate bulk and the deep ridge created by the depth of several layers lying together. The seam will then lie flatter. The widest layer should always be the one resting against the main fabric.

In the case of a jacket with a lapel, the layering will change direction at the break point i.e. the point at which the lapel turns back. Interlined garments do not always require layering, since part of the interlining function is to eliminate the bulk and ridges caused by seam allowances. Check before layering.

PIPING CORD

COVERED PIPING CORD
(Floral Suit, page 30)
Use cotton piping cord and pre-wash to allow for any shrinkage. Polyester cord is hard-wearing but can wear your fabric from the inside out.

Fabric used for covering the cord must be cut on the true bias. If covering very long lengths of cord, you may have to join the bias strips. Ensure the join is also on the true bias (*fig.1*).

First, you must line the piping cord to give a much smoother appearance, to eliminate ridges and twisting. It will also add density to light coloured fabrics. Do not try to cover the cord with lining and fabric at the same time. It will not give the desired effect.

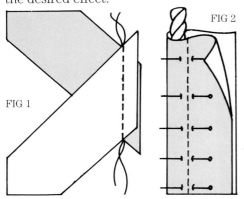

FIG 2

FIG 1

1. Cut 5cm (2in) wide bias strips of lining material of sufficient length to cover the cord. Sandwich the cord between the strip of lining, folding raw edges together. Place pins through the lining into the cord to prevent movement (*fig.2*). Tacking will not secure the cord.
2. Machine 3mm (¹/₈in) from the cord, using a piping foot on the sewing machine.

Now repeat exactly the same process with the main fabric. When covered with both fabrics, the seam allowance can be trimmed to 15mm (⁵/₈in).

TURNING CORNERS WITH PIPING CORD
1. Pin the covered cord in place, resting the cord over the seam allowance towards the main garment.
2. Take the cord to the corner and place a pin at the exact point you wish to turn the cord. Snip into the seam allowance up to the stitching line, at right angles to the pin (*fig.1*).

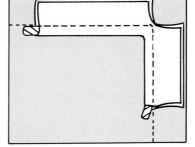

FIG 1

FIG 2

3. Pivot and continue with the cord around the corner (*fig.2*).
4. Machine 3mm (¹/₈in) away from the piping cord, securing the cord to the main garment.

Now the piping cord is ready to be 'sandwiched' with the next layer. If the next layer is a facing or collar, you should stitch 1.5mm (¹/₁₆in) away from the cord so that the previous stitching line remains invisible.

ROULEAUX/FABRIC LOOPS

Use to make a decorative edging, beautiful tiny loops for button fastening, shoe string straps or hanging loops. Loops can easily be made as narrow as 3mm (¹/₈in), using a tool such as the Newey Rouleau Loop Turner/Dritz Loop Turner. All you need are bias cut strips of fabric; use scraps from your garment material.
1. Cut a bias strip 13mm (¹/₂in) wider than finished width and to the required length. Fold the strip in half, lengthways, with right sides together.
2. Keeping the fold edge to the right of the machine, stitch a line the required finished width of your strap, starting with the first few stitches wider than you require. This will make it easier to turn the loop.
3. Now machine a second line just outside the first and trim off immediately next to this, thereby preventing the loop from fraying and forming a seam allowance to pad the loop (*fig.1*).
4. Now turn the loop right side out, using the tool and following the manufacturer's instructions.
5. If you do not have a tool, use a blunt

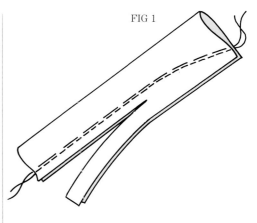

FIG 1

needle and heavy thread. Securely attach the thread to one end of the loop and then push the needle, eye first, through the loop. As you ease the needle along, the fabric will be pulled to the right side.
6. Once the strip is turned right side out, pin one end to the ironing board. Roll it between thumb and forefinger until the stitching line is lying down one side. Stretch slightly and lightly hover over it with the iron – the plate should barely touch the fabric.

The rouleau loop should now be nice and smooth, with no twisting and is ready to use in your garment. Check the length first, since the fabric may have stretched in the process.

THE RUCHED BODICE

In the past I have been somewhat disappointed with the finished effects of ruching. I've come to the conclusion that to do it well a lot of fabric is required. More is better! This may seem costly, but remember, that extra fabric will immediately add a luxurious couture finish.

Follow the technique described here and you will be able to ruche fabric onto any shape – from a simple fichu neckline to the shell shapes on the Beautiful Pink Ballgown (page 86). *Recommended fabrics for ruching:* Any fine fabrics, such as chiffon, georgette, crepe de chine and organza.

Front Bodice
Take a square of the fabric you intend to ruche. If, for example, the fabric is 115cm (45in) wide, you will need that in length.

Now turn this square 45 degrees so that you now have the true bias (*fig.1*). Press a light foldline from top to bottom. Place a pin in the centre.

We now have to find the middle point of the bodice (*fig.2*). Taking the completed front section (Centre Front and Side Front panels) of the boned bodice, find the widest point (line A). In

FIG 1

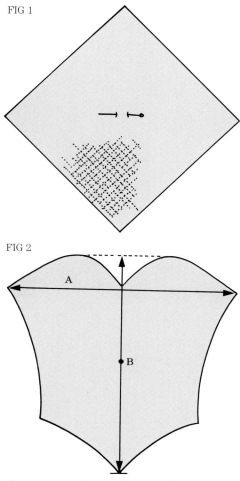

FIG 2

FIG 3

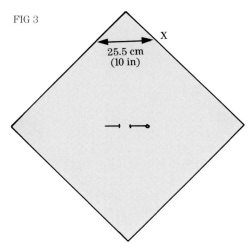

FIG 4

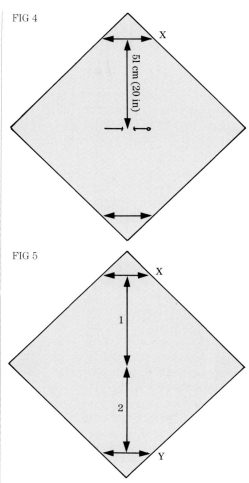

FIG 5

51 cm (20 in)

25.5 cm (10 in)

the case of a basic strapless, boned bodice, it is across the bust. Using the centre point of line A measure from the highest point of the bodice to the lowest. Mark the centre (B).

Take the measurement of A to the bias fabric and find the equivalent measurement, across the width. For example, if it were 25.5cm (10in), it would be as shown on *fig.3*, line X. The fabric beyond this point will be waste since it is not wide enough to be placed on the bodice.

Now measure from the centre point on the bias fabric to point X (*fig.4*). Mark this same distance from the centre downwards (*fig.5* – line Y). Again, fabric beyond Y will be waste because it

is not wide enough for the bodice. Do not cut the waste fabric at this point. The fabric remaining will now ruche evenly onto the bodice because you know:
i) The middle point of the bias and the middle of the bodice;
ii) The highest point on the bias and the highest point of the bodice;
iii) The lowest point on the bias fabric and the lowest point on the bodice.

Hand sew one row of running stitches along either side of the foldline from Y to X using Kinkame thread. I would use a running stitch approximately 6mm (¼in) in length for fine ruching. Leave both thread ends free at the top, in order to gather the fabric (*fig.6*).

FIG 6

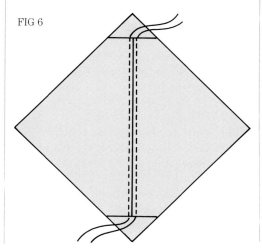

Place the chiffon square over the bodice front, matching the centre points, ensuring the true bias is in line with the straight grain of the bodice.

RUCHING
Pull up the gathering threads so that the lowest point of the square (Y) is level with the lowest point of the bodice, and the top point of the square (X) is in line with the top point of the bodice. Using extra long, extra fine pins, pin in place between every pleat or gather.

Using Kinkame thread (matching the colour of the chiffon) and a fine Straw needle, prickstitch in between every gather that has formed. Remove running threads.
Note: If the prickstitches are too far apart then the ruching will be more widely spaced.

Now, pulling the chiffon gently but quite firmly to maintain the true bias, take the gathers over the bust to the boned seam and pin all the tiny pleats in place. Prickstitch again in between every pin. Repeat for other side of bodice front.

With the fabric firmly in hand, take it towards the side seam. Pin in tiny pleats half-way between the boned seam and the side seam. Prickstitch again (*fig.7*).

Continue to take the chiffon to the side seam; pin and prickstitch. Cut away excess fabric beyond the raw edge of the side seam. Baste the chiffon to the bodice along the top and bottom edges. Trim away any excess chiffon.

FIG 7

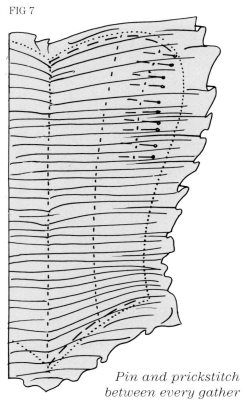

*Pin and prickstitch
between every gather*

Back Bodice

The technique is the same, except that it is done in two separate halves.

Take another bias chiffon square and find the same measurements as you did for the front bodice. Once marked, cut the chiffon square in half from top to bottom (*fig.8*).

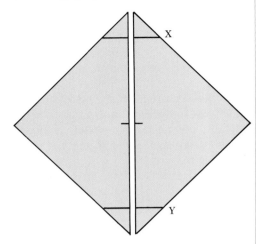

Gather the Centre Back seam as before, using hand sewn running stitches of Kinkame thread but this time place the gathering about 2.5cm (1in) in from the raw edge to accommodate the zip. The gathering line will be placed on the Centre Back foldline of the bodice.

Working one side at a time, gather the chiffon onto the Back bodice, prickstitching in place. Take the pleats over to the boned middle seam. Pin and prickstitch into place. Continue to take the pleats over to a point mid-way between the boned seam and the side seam. Pin and prickstitch in place. Carry the pleats over to the side seam, pin and prickstitch. Trim the excess.

Tack all the way round the outer edges of the bodice, securing the chiffon ruching. Repeat with other bodice Back.

Continue with the boned bodice instructions or your pattern instructions.

SHADOW WORK WITH BEADED POCKETS

(Ivy Leaf Dress, page 74)

Shadow work is a traditional technique often combined with embroidery. Fine opaque fabrics are used with extra layers of fabric or embroidery stitched behind to create a shadow effect from the front.

I have used this method in the *Ivy Leaf Dress.* Here the shadow work consists of two layers of ivory coloured organza. A trellis design has been embroidered with pure silk thread, then alternate blocks of the skirt trellis work

have been cut away from the underlayer of organza; thus two layers of organza will be lying next to a single layer, giving the shadow effect. To complete the design I have embroidered an ivy leaf pattern, using the two layers of organza to form small pockets all around the hemline, which have been filled with tiny beads (see photo below).

You will need:

Embroidery needle.

Madeira 4 Strand Pure Silk embroidery thread (use only two strands at a time).

Two layers of organza.

Small beads (I used ivory and peach shades. The quantity for each pocket will be dependent on the bead size and your own personal choice).

Mount the two organza layers together and tack around all edges. Use light pencil marks to transfer your design to the organza. Refer to the construction method below for the trellis work before transferring the design. Note that the trellis design does not extend beyond the embroidered border design. Complete the border embroidery first, then you will know where to finish the trellis.

BORDER EMBROIDERY AND BEADED POCKETS

1. It is helpful to draw your design around the hemline first, using a light pencil line.

2. Take the needle and embroidery thread (2 strands) and use a small backstitch (about 3mm/$^1/_8$in) to sew around the design, stitching through both layers of fabric.

3. The bead pockets have been formed from the two layers of organza in the ivy leaf embroidery. Start by backstitching the bottom half of each leaf design with embroidery thread to form a cup shape. Pour some of the beads into the cup.

4. Carry on stitching the leaf shape to completely enclose the beads. Now re-stitch the design within the first stitching line to form a smaller version of the design, manoeuvring all the beads to the centre (see photo). Complete all the bead pockets and lower embroidery panel before starting the trellis design using Shadow Work.

SHADOW WORK

When first applying a trellis, block or diamond design to fabric it is very important to keep it absolutely symmetrical, which can be difficult. The best way is to work in a square.

1. For example, take the front skirt panel of the Ivy Leaf Dress, that is, the two layers of organza worked as one.

ABOVE: Trellis design and bead-filled ivy leaf pockets

Use a Straw needle and Kinkame thread to tack a straight line denoting the Centre Front (A). Measure the line from highest point to hemline. We shall say it measures 51cm (20in). Halve this figure (25.5cm/10in) and measure out this distance either side of line A, giving lines B and C (*fig.1*).

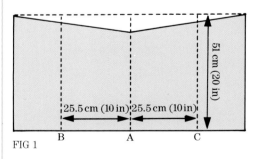

FIG 1

You now have a square. Mark the diagonal lines by bringing the opposite corners together. Backstitch along these lines first. The centre point of your square will be where the two diagonals cross (*fig.2*).

2. To form the symmetrical trellis design you now simply draw a parallel line 5cm (2in) from the diagonals. Stitch in place and then draw further parallel lines until you have completed

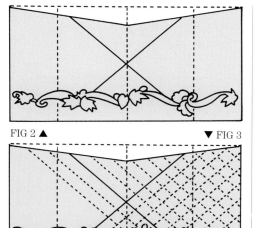

FIG 2 ▲   ▼ FIG 3

the lower skirt edge (*fig.3*).

3. Working from the underlayer of organza, use a very small pair of scissors to snip into the lower layer only, in the area you wish to remove. Cut carefully, close to the stitches, avoiding the top layer of organza entirely. Remove the shape from the under layer.

In the trellis design I have removed diamond shapes at random. If you were using a flower design, you could cut out alternate petals or leaves to give depth or shadow.

SLEEVES

SETTING IN SLEEVES

I spent many years trying different methods of setting-in sleeves, ending up with all the usual problems such as puckering and tiny tucks. Through trial and error I came up with this technique which never fails me.

1. Machine stitch one row of large stitches (gathering stitch) between the front and back armhole notches. On fine fabrics where the stitching holes will be seen, ensure that you stitch immediately next to the seam allowance line (i.e. just under 15mm (⅝in) from the raw edge).

When working with wool or linen, this line can be sewn on the other side of the stitching line, on the sleeve side. This will form a breakline so that when the stitches are gathered up, the ease allowance will start to disappear. The earlier the breakline on the sleeve head, the earlier you start to loose the ease, and the easier it will be to set in the sleeve.

2. Pin in the sleeve with right sides together, matching up shoulder points, underarm seams, front and back notches. Pull up the gathering thread so that the sleeve sits comfortably in the armhole. Now remove the pins and take out the sleeve, keeping the gathered

line pulled up. Holding the sleeve upright, place it on the ironing board and steam the inside head of the sleeve to set the ease permanently in place.

3. Pin the sleeve back in place, matching up points as before. Place a few extra pins on the stitching line in the direction that you will sew.

4. Place the garment under the machine, starting to stitch at the underarm seam. With the sleeve uppermost, stitch on the seam line (*fig.1*).

FIG 1

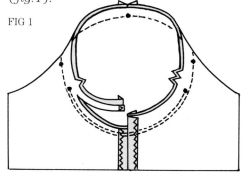

Reinforce and trim the underarm seam area only

Machine slowly around the top of the sleeve. If any little tucks start to appear use the tip of a pin to push them back towards the seam allowance. You might also find that an extra tug, stretching the sleeve into the armhole will work too but do make sure the machine foot is down and the needle in the fabric.

This method really works well on interlined garments because the interlayers make everything more stable. Notice there is no tacking. I find this too restricting; tacking can often cause more problems.

5. Now machine a second line, 6mm (¼in) from the seam line, on the seam allowance from the front notch down to the underarm seam and up to the back notch (*fig.1*). On the underarm section only of the seam, trim off excess fabric and clip. This will give extra comfort during wear.

You are now ready to put in the sleeve head.

SLEEVE HEADS

All set-in sleeves need a sleeve head. The top of the sleeve is a continuation of the shoulder area and you should therefore create a smooth line. Problems often occur due to the fullness eased into the seam allowance which rests against the main fabric, causing a dimpled or wrinkled effect.

A sleeve head will keep the two apart, giving a smooth, soft roundness to the head of the sleeve. This also works wonders when ironing as it creates a

built-in pressing pad! To make sleeve heads for any garment in this book you require only a strip of 2oz wadding or needlepoint felt.

1. Measure the sleeve head between the back and front notches of the armhole. Add on 13mm (½in) to both ends. Cut a strip of wadding to this length, 5cm (2in) wide.

2. Place the sleeve head flat down to the top of the sleeve so that 13mm (½in) lays over the seam allowance; the remaining 3.8cm (1½in) is in the sleeve and the ends extend 13mm (½in) beyond each notch. Place pins horizontally across the seam.

3. Turn the garment over so that the sleeve head is underneath and the machine stitching which joins the sleeve to the armhole is visible. Now machine 1.5mm (1/16in) from the original stitching line, in the seam allowance (*fig.1*). Remove the pins as you go. Trim the wadding so that it is level with the seam allowance at both ends and only 2.5cm (1in) wide at the shoulder seam (*fig.2*).

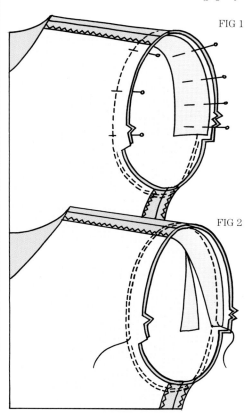

FIG 1

FIG 2

4. Turn sleeve to the right side. Place your hand inside and gently steam over the roundness of the shoulder and sleeve head.

SHOULDER PADS (for set-in sleeves)
You will need:

1 pair of medium, uncovered sponge pads.

0.45m (½yd) light wadding to provide softness without too much bulk.

0.45m (½yd) muslin to cover the pad (use muslin rather than lining as it will not slip or fill with air).

Shoulder pads need to be individually made since no two shoulders are the same. The purpose of the pad is to fill the gap between you and the garment, giving shape and body. Without sufficient support the shoulders will collapse and ruin the line of the garment. You can control the build by the quantity of foundation and the position within the pad.

Small-shouldered people will find that, if there is a gap from the top shoulder bone, there will also be a gap toward the front and back of the shoulders. I always make my shoulder pads the same length as the distance between the back and front notches on the armhole. This may look very long for a shoulder pad, but it is really what is required. Creating such a pad will eliminate those droopy lines that often occur from the neck to the armhole.

1. First you need a good solid foundation. Take one sponge pad. If you need extra height place a smaller pad on top of it. If this is too much, cut a piece of wadding slightly smaller than the medium-sized pad. Keep trimming until you have the required height.

2. You will need a pattern for covering the pad. Do this by measuring between the front and back notch on the armhole (A–B). Measure along the shoulder line from the raw edge at the armhole to within 2.5cm (1in) of the inside neck edge (C–D).

Draw in a nice curve from A through to C and on to B. This is your pattern piece, placing the straight line A–B on the fold (*fig.1*).

FIG 1

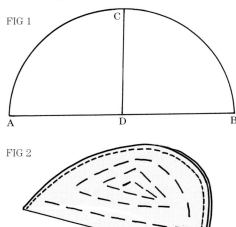

FIG 2

3. Cut two of these in wadding. Cut two in muslin; on the bias and 13mm (½in) larger all the way round the outer edge.
4. Sandwich the sponge pad inside the

wadding then cover with muslin.
5. Machine all the way round the outer edge. Tack through the pad to keep all layers together. Do not pull the stitches too tight. Remember, you want to keep the height (*fig.2*).

Setting in the Pad
1. Lay the middle of the shoulder pad over the shoulder seam, bringing it down to meet the raw edge of the seam allowance at the armhole edge.
2. Hand stitch through the seam allowance and all thicknesses of the pad 13mm (½in) from the raw edge, securing the pad to the garment. Do not pull tight, maintain the height. Only stitch along the top 11.3cm (4½in) of the sleeve head, 5.6cm (2¼in) either side of the shoulder seam. Remember, these shoulder pads are longer than usual. Allow the two ends to hang free, otherwise they will pull every time you move your arms.
3. Bar tack, by hand, the shoulder pad to the seam allowance at the neck edge.

WAISTBAND
This technique is suitable for all straight waistbands, up to 7.5cm (3in) in depth.
You will need:
Main fabric cut to the required length (including seam allowances).
One length of soft, fine fusible interfacing.
One length of belt backing without any seam allowances.

The use of belt backing (e.g. Dura-bac) will eliminate many of the usual problems encountered with waistbands. Dura-bac is very firm and comfortable but do avoid using a band that is too deep for you. A narrow waistband can become quite bulky due to all the layers resting against it. With this technique they will be behind the belt backing, giving a perfectly smooth finish from the front. You will also be able to achieve a perfect edge to edge finish at the back, with both ends the same depth.

I recommend a hook and eye to complete, since buttonholes can be quite difficult in all the bulk of the waistband.

1. Press the interfacing to the wrong side of the main fabric waistband to strengthen it and prevent any show-through from the belt backing.
2. Machine the interlined waistband to the top of the skirt (right sides together), taking a 15mm (⅝in) seam allowance. A skirt will usually have an underlap on the Right Back. Keep right

sides together so that both waistband and the seam allowances remain as shown in *fig.1*.

FIG 1

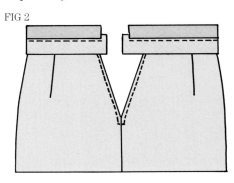

3. Place the belt backing wrong side down to the seam allowance, with the lower edge resting just above the stitching line (*fig.2*).

Ensure the backing stops 15mm (⅝in) from both ends of the waistband because there are no seam allowances for the backing. Edgestitch the backing in place by machine.

FIG 2

4. Press the seam allowance on the long, unstitched edge of the waistband to the wrong side. Turn in the raw ends of the waistband.

Now fold the band over the belt backing, bringing the fold-edge down to conceal the stitching line. As you bring it down, tuck the pressed seam allowance under the folded edge of the waistband end. This forms a neat finish. Repeat at the other end of the waistband.
5. Pin the folded edge in place along the stitching line and slipstitch in place. Complete with a covered hook and bar (see technique detailed earlier).

FIG 3

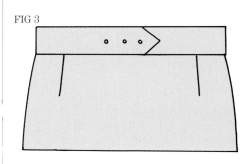

You could make a feature of the waistband by giving the appearance of a built-in belt. Instead of having an underlap, have an overlap and mitre the belt backing to give a belt effect (*fig.3*). Finish with false buttons for detail and secure with hook and eye fastener.

BUILT-IN WAISTBAND

Use this technique for heavy gowns, particularly those with a boned bodice, to avoid any downward pull.

1. Cut a length of waistband ribbon the exact, comfortable waist measurement plus 5cm (2in). Fold back 2.5cm (1in) at either end and machine. This will allow for any adjustments required.

2. Line up the ribbon on the inside of the bodice at waist level and hand stitch strongly through the waistband into the lining, then through to the seam allowances of the bodice. Stitch at the side seams and middle back seams, leaving it hanging free from this point.

3. Stitch a large hook and eye to the ends of the waistband, so that you finish with the band edge to edge and the hook and eye on the outside of the band; this will ensure the band is flat to the waist.

ZIGZAG FINISH

Used on fine fabrics, which have not been interlined, to give a neat finish to the seam allowance.

1. Machine stitch the usual 15mm (⅝in) seam allowance.

2. Machine a second row 6mm (¼in) from the first stitching line. Trim up to this second row of stitching.

3. Set your machine to a small, fairly open zigzag stitch. Place the centre mark of the basic machine foot on the second row of stitching. Zigzag on and off this line.

The second row of stitching will stabilize the zigzag, giving it something to roll around. The result will be a much more even stitch.

ZIP PLACEMENT

Follow this technique for skirt, dress and bodice zips.

1. Fold back the seam allowance (2.5cm/1in) on both sides of the zip opening. Remember, I recommend a larger seam allowance to accommodate the zip. Press lightly.

2. With right side uppermost place the zip teeth, right side up, under the fold-line of the right side. The top of the zip should lie about 6mm (¼in) below the top edge and only the teeth should be visible (*fig.1*). Hold in place with just a few pins through all layers. Turn the fabric to the wrong side and now pin the zip to the seam allowance only,

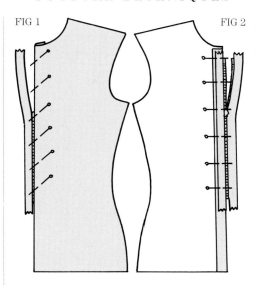

FIG 1   FIG 2

removing pins from the right side of garment as you work (*fig.2*).

3. Open out the seam allowance flat and machine close to the right-hand side of the teeth, allowing room for the zip tongue to pass. Machine from the bottom of the zip to the top (*fig.3*).

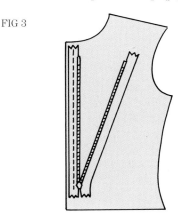

FIG 3

For bodice zip: Begin approximately 5cm (2in) from the bottom of the bodice to allow for the skirt attachment at a later stage.

When the seam allowance is folded back to the wrong side again, only the teeth and left side of the zip will be visible (*fig.1*).

4. Close the zip. With right sides uppermost, position the left-hand side to completely cover the zip and extend over the right-hand side by 6mm (¼in). Top edges should be level. Hold the zip in place on the left side with just a few pins through all the layers. This time, the zip teeth should lie further back from the fold edge (*fig.4*).

For bodice zip: Match the canvas edge, not the raw edge.

5. Open zip fully. Take the left side and transfer the pins to the wrong side as you did before, fixing the zip to the seam allowance only. Open the seam allowance flat and machine, stitching from top to bottom.

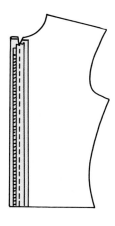

FIG 4

For bodice zip: Finish about 5cm (2in) from the lower edge of the bodice.

By overlapping the edges of the zip opening, you will create an ease allowance; when the garment is worn the edges will not gape.

6. Use this stage only for a dress with a top neck facing, a bodice or a skirt having an inner waistband of petersham or similar.

Fold the seam allowances back to the wrong side of the garment. Now snip 15mm (⅝in) down from the top edge just in line to where the zip teeth start (*fig.4*). Do not snip any further.

Open the seam allowance and fold down the seam allowance between the two clips you have created (*fig.5*). Fold the zip seam allowance back to the wrong side and continue with the next step.

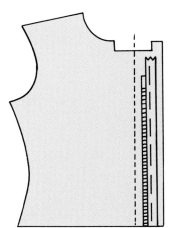

FIG 5

7. Now secure the zip, by prickstitching in place through all layers. On the left side stitch 15mm (⅝in) from the outer edge, taking care not to stitch right next to the teeth as this will tend to make the fabric stand up rather than lie flat. On the right side make the stitches 3mm (⅛in) from the edge. Make the stitches about 13mm (½in) apart so that they are not too close together.

For bodice zip: Overstitch the seam allowances of the zip down to the interlining layer, to within 7.5cm (3in) of the lower edge.

The following stitches have all been used in the construction of the collection.

BACKSTITCH

This stitch is used for embroidery purposes on the Ivy Leaf Dress (page 74). It forms a strong, solid line.

Bring the needle up to the right side of fabric at X and make a running stitch backwards. Bring the needle back up one full stitch length in front of X. Take one running stitch backwards to fill the gap and continue. Use a stitch length of approximately 2–3mm ($^1/_6$–$^1/_8$in).

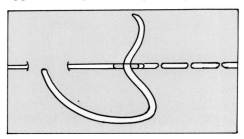

BAR TACK

Strengthen buttonholes at each end with this technique.

Take approximately four stitches across the depth of the buttonhole at each end, then work a blanket stitch over these stitches.

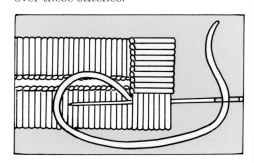

BLANKET STITCH

As the name suggests, an edging stitch which can be used in bar tacks (above), belt carriers and other hand-sewn finishes. Work from left to right with the edge to be stitched facing you.

Using a small needle, secure the thread to the fabric edge. Push the needle from right side to wrong side, about 6mm ($^1/_4$in) from the edge and the needle pointing towards you.

Ensure the thread is under the needle before pulling the needle completely through. Repeat the process, making the stitches fairly close together.

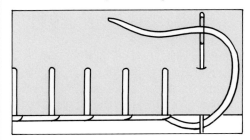

BLINDSTITCH

This stitch is hidden from view when worked between two layers, such as hems and facings.

Turn down the upper fabric approximately 6mm ($^1/_4$in) and make a small diagonal stitch, catching one thread of the lower fabric. Now make a small diagonal stitch back to the upper fabric. Continue in this way.

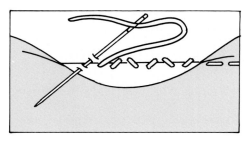

BUTTONHOLE STITCH

For a lovely, hand-finished buttonhole (see Couture Techniques) use a pure silk Gütermann thread on fine to medium weight fabrics; for heavier fabrics use a button twist or strong tailoring thread.

Mark the buttonhole area with a machine zigzag line first. Secure the thread to the wrong side, half-way along the buttonhole length, using the machine zigzag line as a guide.

Insert the needle through the opening of the buttonhole, pushing the needle through to the right side. With the needle still in the fabric, wrap the thread around the needle to form a loop. Pull up the needle so that a knot is formed at the buttonhole edge. Continue around the opening, ensuring

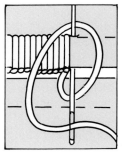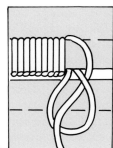

that each knot lies on the hole edge and that stitches are of an even length. Form an arch at either end of the buttonhole by fanning out the stitches. Strengthen the sides of the hole with a bar tack worked on the wrong side.

CROSS STITCH

A strong stitch which is worked in two different directions. May be used to join interfacings together or where some stress may be present in a joined seam. Cross stitch eliminates the bulk of trying to turn in a raw edge and when covered gives a flat finish. It can be used as a decorative finish to pleats in tailored linings.

Insert the needle parallel to the seam and stitch diagonally along the seam. Return in the same manner, crossing over the first line of stitches.

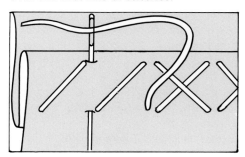

GATHERING STITCH

All gathering featured in this book will be worked by machine. This gives a stronger gathering thread since you have two threads rather than the single, hand-worked thread

Adjust your machine to the longest stitch length. Machine one row almost on the seam allowance line. Make a second and third row of stitching above this line, but all within the seam

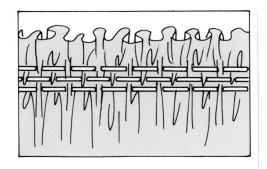

allowance. If working on a large gathered skirt, divide the skirt into four sections. Gather up each section separately, pulling up all three threads.

HERRINGBONE STITCH

This stitch will give a flat finish but also a certain degree of give. Suitable for hems and securing interfacings. Work from left to right.

Make a small horizontal stitch in the main fabric. Now move diagonally to the right of this stitch and make another small horizontal stitch in the second fabric. Take the thread back up to the main fabric, again working in diagonal lines. As you work the stitches will cross over. Do not pull the stitches too tight.

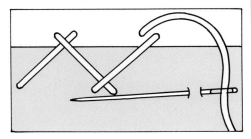

LADDER STITCH

Used to stitch a seam together from the front when it is too awkward or impossible to stitch from behind. You will find it used on the deep points of the collars and revers in the Pink Appliquéd Suit.

Take a small stitch across from one side of the seam to the other. Make a hidden running stitch, then cross over to the other side. Work about 13mm (½in) at a time, then pull up the stitches to create the ladder which firmly closes the seam.

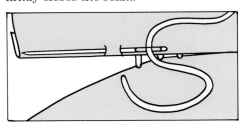

OVERSEWING/OVERCAST STITCH

Used to secure one layer to another, such as seam to interlining. Can also be used to define an edge and to flatten bulk from behind. This should be a firm, strong stitch.

Take a strong, double thread. Secure it to the seam and make a diagonal stitch of about 10mm (³/₈in) over the edge. Make a small horizontal stitch into the fabric, coming back up into the seam ready for the next stitch.

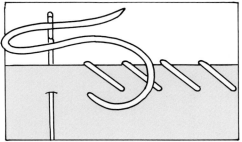

PRICKSTITCH

A strong stitch where only a very small stitch is visible from the front. I have used it around the zip area to secure the zip in place.

This stitch is often used to keep facings and linings towards the wrong side, rather than allowing them to roll towards the right side of the garment.

Work prickstitch in the same manner as backstitch, but keep the stitches on the upper surface as tiny as possible, literally the size of a pinhead.
For the zip area: Bring the needle up through all layers. Make a tiny backstitch on the top surface, going under and bringing the needle back to the top again about 13mm (½in) in front of the last one. When securing facings and linings the understitch does not go through all layers, but through to the interlining layer only.

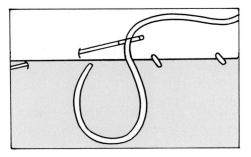

SLIPSTITCH

This stitch will give an almost invisible finish. Ideal for attaching lining to a waistband and for hand-worked, bound buttonholes.

Make a running stitch through the folded fabric, emerge directly below this point and make a tiny stitch to the lower fabric. Take the needle immediately back up into the folded fabric and repeat. The only visible stitch will be the tiny 'v' stitch which joins the two edges together.

STAYSTITCH

Used on bias or curved areas before they are joined together, to prevent them stretching out of shape.

Worked by hand (running stitch) or machine, it is a row of even stitches approximately 13mm (½in) from the raw edge and always within the seam allowance area.

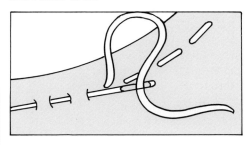

TACKING OR BASTING

This is a temporary stitch, used to keep more than one layer of fabric in place until it is permanently stitched or secured. Work it as a continuous, even running stitch, with a 13mm (½in) space between each 13mm (½in) stitch.

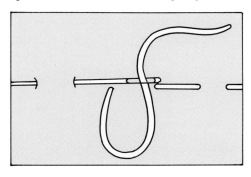

ZIGZAG STITCH

Most, if not all, basic sewing machines have the facility for a zigzag stitch. Refer to your machine manual for information on uses and stitch widths/lengths.

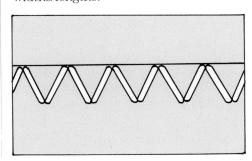

Here you will find definitions of all fabrics used in the collection. Some fabric names will vary internationally; this glossary is intended to give guidance in locating the equivalent fabrics. We also include explanations for several dressmaking terms, which less-experienced sewers may find helpful.

BONING
Provides shape and support for strapless garments, costumes and bustiers. Usually available in black or white.

BREMSILK
A man-made, anti-static lining of very high quality. Ideal for lining pure silks, especially chiffon and crepe de chine. If seeking an alternative for Bremsilk, avoid the use of polyester or nylon linings.

CANVAS
A heavy, firm, strong fabric often made of cotton or acrylic. Produced in many grades and qualities.

CHIFFON
A sheer, very lightweight, plain-weave fabric.

CREPE
Any fabric with a puckered, crinkled or grainy surface. Crepe fabrics include chiffon, crepe-backed satin, georgette wool crepe and crepe de chine.

CREPE DE CHINE
A lightweight, opaque, plain-weave, filament-yarn, having a medium lustre. Silk crepe de chine is usually made with crepe yarns.

DOMETTE/DOMET/DOMETT
A fabric having cotton warp and wool weft, similar to flannelette.

DOUPION/DUPION
An irregular, raw, rough silk reeled from double cocoons.

DUCHESSE SATIN
Thicker than ordinary satin, this does not drape like a silk satin but will mould and maintain a lofty effect.

DUCK
A closely woven, plain-weave fabric similar to canvas, usually made from cotton or linen yarns. The names canvas and duck have become almost generic and are usually qualified by terms that indicate the use of the fabric, for example artist's canvas and duck linen.

GROSGRAIN
A ribbed fabric, traditionally made from pure silk. The fabric is quite stiff, with lots of body. The rib is wider than that found in Poult, but not as wide or heavy as Ottoman. Grosgrain is also woven as a narrow ribbon.

HABUTAI
A lightweight, soft silk fabric imported from Japan, hence the alternative name of Jap silk. It is of a heavier weight than China silk.

HOLLAND
1. Originally a fine, plain-woven linen fabric, made in many European countries but especially in Holland.
2. A plain, medium-weight cloth of cotton or linen with a beetled or glazed finish.

HORSEHAIR BRAID
Used to stiffen and support hem edges.

INTERFACING
A fabric used to stabilize and stiffen key areas of a garment, such as collars and cuffs. Interfacings can either be sewn into the garment or fused to the main fabric with heat.

INTERLINING/UNDERLINING
An optional, additonal layer(s) which works as one with the main fabric. Used to structure and mould the main fabric or to balance fabrics of different weights. Refer to 'Before You Begin . . .' on page 9 for further information.

LACE
There are many different laces, often named after the place of origin. Cotton and silk laces are of a far superior quality.

LAWN
A fine, plain-woven cloth of linen or cotton made in various fine, sheer qualities. Various finishes may be applied to a fabric of this type.
   Lawn finish is a light starch applied to lawn and other fine yarn plain fabrics to give a crisp finished material.

MULL
A plain cotton fabric of relatively open texture. Made from fine yarn, it is soft-finished and usually bleached.

MUSLIN
A generic term for a lightweight, open cloth of plain weave. Some of these cloths are used in the 'grey/griege', for example cheesecloth, but dress muslins are bleached and dyed.

NAP
A fabric is said to have a nap when part of the fibre has been raised from the basic structure. The words nap and pile are often used synonymously.

ORGANZA
Transparent, crisp, lightweight plain-weave fabric made of filament yarns.

PETERSHAM RIBBON/WAISTBAND RIBBON
A narrow fabric which has a pronounced rib and a stiffness along the length, which is produced by the high density weave or a finishing process. It has an edge of contrasting weave. May be more familiar as Waistband with Stiffener, Banrol or Armoflex.

POULT
A plain-weave fabric which belongs to a group of fabrics having a rib in the weft direction. This group includes taffeta, faille and grosgrain. Poult was originally known as Poult de Soie. Poult lining can be likened to a 100% taffeta lining with a pronounced rib.

SATIN
A strong, lustrous, medium to heavy weight satin weave fabric.

SELVEDGE/SELVAGE
The longitudinal bound edges of the fabric which are formed during weaving. After final processing these edges are gripped by hooks to stretch the fabric back into an even width along the roll. Selvedges may differ from the main body of the fabric; some carry brand names or fabric descriptions which are woven or printed into them. Their main purpose is to prevent fraying and to give strength to the fabric during weaving.

SILK
The protein fibre forming cocoons spun by the silkworm. Pure silk contains no metallic or other weighting of any kind, except that which is essential to the dyeing process.

TAFFETA
A general term referring to plain-weave, closely woven, smooth and crisp fabric with a faint weft-way rib; produced from filament yarns.

THAI TAFFETA
A good quality, fine silk from Thailand. Quite light but firmly woven.

TULLE/NET
There are different varieties and weights including:
Tulle the finest; a soft, very lightweight, machine-made net. Dress-weight net is of medium weight, used for adding froth and fullness to a garment. Stiff net is the firmest and is used for sculpturing a garment.

WADDING/BATTING
A soft bonded material used to pad and quilt. Available in various weights.

Anchor Threads:
Coats Patons Crafts
McMullen Road
Darlington
Co Durham DL1 1YQ
Tel 0325 381010

Coats & Clark Inc
Coats Crafts North America
30 Patwood Drive
Suite 351
Greenville SC29615, USA

DMC Threads:
DMC Creative World
Pulham Road
Wigston
Leicestershire LE18 2DY
Tel 0533 811040

DMC Corporation
Port Kearny
Building 10
South Kearny
NJ 07032, USA

Gütermann Threads:
Perivale-Gütermann Ltd
Wadsworth Road
Greenford
Middlesex UB6 7JS
Tel 081 998 5000

Gütermann of America Inc
PO Box 7387
Charlotte NC 28241, USA
Tel (704) 525 7068

Kinkame Thread:
distributed by Tootalcraft (UK),
Mölnlycke (rest of Europe) and
Britex, San Francisco, USA.

Tootalcraft
Unit 1 & 2 Clarence Avenue
Ashburton
Trafford Park
Manchester M17 1QS
Tel 061 872 9889

Madeira Threads:
Madeira Threads (UK) Ltd
PO Box 6
Thirsk
North Yorkshire
Y07 3YX

Madeira Marketing Ltd
600 East 9th Street
Michigan City IN 46360
USA

Madeira Garne
U & M Schmidt u Co GmbH
Postfach 320
D-79003 Freiburg
Germany

UK Metal Threads:
Benton & Johnson Ltd
26 Marshalsea Road
London SE1 1HF
Tel 071 407 8646

USA Metal Threads:
Kreinik Mfg Co Inc
9199 Reisterstown Road
Suite 209B
Owings Mills
MD 21117, USA
Tel 1-800-537-2166
Fax (410) 581-5092

UK Beads:
Ells & Farrier
20 Beak Street
London W1R 3PH
Tel 071 629 9964

Bead products; reference codes
M15, M12, M25 and SB10, colour
30.

Threads, notions and fabrics:
The John Lewis Partnership
Oxford Street
London W1A 1EX
Tel (071) 629 7711
(phone for nearest branch)

Newey Goodman Ltd
Sedgley Road West
Tipton
West Midlands DY4 8AH
Tel 021 522 2500

Dritz Corporation
Box 5028
Spartanburg SC 29304, USA

*Bondaweb®/Wonder
Under®/Vliesofix®/Vilene®
Volume Fleece 280/Pellon
Fleece:*
Freudenberg Nonwovens Ltd
Vilene Retail
PO Box 3, Greetland
Halifax HX4 8NJ
West Yorkshire
Tel (0422)313131

Vliesofix®:
Carl Freudenberg
6940 Weinheim/Bergstrasse
Postfach 1369
Germany

Wonder Under®:
Freuden Nonwovens Ltd
Pellon Division
1040 Avenue of the Americas
New York NY 100018, USA

Dura-bac® Belting:
Staflex Products Ltd
137 Church Road
Potters Bar
Hertfordshire EN6 1EU

Our thanks for assistance in
compiling the fabric glossary to:
American Textile Manufacturer's
Institute
Fabric Sourcing Division
1801 K Street NW
Suite 900
Washington DC 20006, USA

and for assistance with the Metal
Thread Embroidery techniques:
Royal School of Needlework
Apartment 12A,
Hampton Court Palace
East Molesey
Surrey KT8 9AU
Tel 081 943 1432

for the Metal Thread design and
embroidery: Hazel Everett

for the provision of plain buttons
and the large covered belt
featured on Design No 1, the
double-bound buttons on Design
No 2 and the gold-edged buttons
on Design No 7;

EA & HM Bull Ltd
Harlequin
Unit 1A Riverside Avenue West
Lawford
Manningtree
Essex CO11 1UX

And finally the author would like
to thank the following people for
their help in the production of
the book: Carey Smith; Rick
Sullivan; Jan Tordoff; Julie
Watkins and Rosemary Wilkinson.

BIBLIOGRAPHY
The Textile Institute Terms and Definitions 9th Edition
The Textile Institute 1991
International Headquarters
10 Blackfriars Street
Manchester M3 5DR

Textiles: Sixth Edition
N Hollen, J Saddler, A L Longford, S J Kadolph
International Edition ISBN 0-02-946270-3
Macmillan Publishing Co (1988)
866 Third Avenue
NY, NY 10022, USA

128

Terry Fox has launched her own company, The English Couture Company, which offers a whole range of tuition in couture techniques, in the form of workshops and courses, as well as supplying a mail order service for specially selected interfacings and interlinings, including all interlinings features in this book. For information, contact the address below:

The English Couture Company
60 Queensberry Avenue
Copford
Colchester
CO6 1YN
United Kingdom

Tel: 0284 878388